WEDLOCKED WOMEN

"I thought I saw two persons coming down the road but it was only a man and his wife."   *Russian proverb*

Feminist Books

A

Published 1974 by Feminist Books Ltd.
P.O. Box HP5
Leeds LS6 1LN
England

Publisher's note

Feminist Books is a new, independent, publishing house with an all-women editorial board. Any profits from the sale of this book will go directly to the financing of further publications from the Women's Liberation Movement in Britain.

Cover designed by Lee Sanders and Ian Tod at HOWCOW (Howden Co-operative Workshop), Bishop's Manor, Howden, Yorkshire.

ISBN 0-904426-00-9 paper
ISBN 0-904426-01-7 cloth

Made and printed in Great Britain by John Blackburn Ltd., Old Run Road, Leeds 10, England.

Contents

Acknowledgments

This book lays no claim to analysing the oppression of women. But I have tried with the help and understanding of the Women's Liberation Movement, to describe the subjection of women, particularly as they experience it in the family, in their role as housewives and mothers.

I have not written this book alone. Many of the ideas in it have come directly from discussions and writings generated by women in the Movement. It's my involvement in that Movement and my commitment to its politics which gave me the impetus to start writing this book and the determination to finish it.

For their friendship, interest, criticisms and advice, for loaning me books, bringing to my attention relevant material and for saving newspaper cuttings, my thanks to Gloden Dallas, John Dennis, Sue Garvin, Anne Geraghty, Hilary Hackett, Robin Harvey, Lis Kustow, Dave Lacey, Louise Lavender, Stephanie Munro, Cammilla Nightingale, Ann Oakley, Jan Savage, Libby Scott, Ann Sutherland, Ian Tod, Jan Wallis, Judith Weymont, Jackie Wootton and members of the Leeds and York Women's Liberation groups.

For their inspiration, insights and emotional support, my love and deepest thanks to Sandra Allen, John Comer and Michelene Wandor. I leaned on them much more than they know and this book is lovingly and appreciatively dedicated to them.

* * * * * * *

Socialisation

Self-Fulfilling Pophecy

> "... man is defined as a human being and woman is defined as a female. Whenever she tries to behave as a human being she is accused of trying to emulate the male ..."
>
> Simone de Beauvoir

OUR children are brought up to believe that the world they inhabit is a natural one and that the divisions between the races, sexes and classes are an inevitable result of human nature. If the world is in a mess, it's because human nature is badly flawed. Space travel, the desecration of the planet, war, exploitation, leader worship and progress, when they're not being extolled by defenders of the status quo, can all be laid at the door of human nature.

Human nature is an all-purpose tool, always available as a last refuge and always a basic tenet of expedient human behaviour. And it's a blind alley. The authors of 'The Naked Ape', 'The Territorial Imperative', 'The Imperial Animal' and 'Men in Groups' all achieved a considerable degree of publicity by focusing our attention on human aggression. We are, so these authors tell us, barely out of the jungle and men are, by nature, aggressive, dominant, hierarchical, status seeking and conquistadorial. Skulls of early human beings showing violent death, warring tribes and the hunting instinct are every man's stock in trade – a symbolic justification for a violent world. As a model of humanity it's irresistible to many people. 'You can't change human nature, you know!'

The tool finds its best purpose when it is used to bolster up patriarchal society. As Elaine Morgan showed

I

in her book 'The Descent of Woman', all speculations on the nature of humanity and its evolution have assumed the human race to be an all male preserve. When the female of the species appears, she's used only as a little light relief to further reflect on the stature of the male. (She's got a fleshy bottom and rounded breasts because the male likes fleshy bottoms and rounded breasts.) When admissible, the female is useful only as a carrier of the species and as a pleasure object. In all else she is presented as a defective male.

Human nature has a lot to answer for. It is now the overburdened beast on which patriarchal society is a grotesque parasite, its resources distorted and sucked dry in the service of its master. And both are now so interdependent that we find it hard to disentangle one from the other. Is it the beast which is responsible for the injustice and oppression in the world or is it the parasite? In any case, it's the last trick up every man's sleeve, making men climb mountains and women climb stairs and making grown men put away childish things and women put away children's things.

Some of these myths form the bread and butter of our experience. Women's liberation, student activists, revolutionary socialists and the hippy movement are all trying, in their very different ways, to explode these myths. They are either dismissed as idealists or they are rewarded with harassment, brutalisation, imprisonment and sometimes death. Radical change and ideals have no place in a world where human nature is deemed to have such a remorseless command of men's sensibilities.

Anthony Storr is an eminent writer and psychiatrist. He, too, joins ranks with those who hold this determinist view of Western society. "Democracy," he says, "is not natural; it has to be learned, protected and cherished; for man's nature is competitive, status-seeking and acquisitive."[1] Is wearing clothes, typing invoices and driving cars *natural*? But it is not my purpose here to take sides or refute his assumptions, (though there is a mass of counter evidence for the generous, peaceful nature of human beings) but merely to show that we are conditioned to behave according to its supposed precepts. As aggression and dominance appear to be largely absent from the female and as the female of the species is also heir to human nature, perhaps Dr. Storr could say that it is aggression which has to be "learned, protected and cherished" and not democracy.

In the final analysis, discussions of the fundamental nature of humanity are so flexible as to be used both to attack and defend the status quo. No appeals to behavioural or determinist theories will ever succeed in unravelling the complexities and contradictions in our society, for, like fish who do not know that they live in water, we are enveloped by its culture.

* * * * * *

In most respects, the human infant is everywhere the same – helpless, capable only of reflex actions and totally dependent on adult care for several years. From these same beginnings human beings grow up to be anything from an Australian Aborigine to an Eskimo, from an assembly-line worker to an aristocrat. The fact that we are all human with the same needs and desires should go without saying. We wear clothes, make love, speak to each other, build houses, grow food, work and provide for our young and old. But the superficial differences appear so marked that many people in the industrialised societies believe that those who are not

3

like them are, for that reason, not quite human. Both the assembly-line worker and the aristocrat regard the other as being of a different breed. So it is worthwhile to remind the aristocrat that, had he been taken at birth and placed in an Eskimo society, he would *be* an Eskimo.

The process by which the human infant is moulded to fit the society into which she or he is born has been called 'socialisation'. The term is loosely defined as the way in which a member of a given society "acquires the values and knowledge of his group and learns the social roles appropriate to his position in it."[2] Women in Western societies (and many other societies) are victims of a pernicious form of socialisation which stamps them at birth with their inferiority. It then attributes that inferiority to their genes. Nowhere is the myth of what is natural more powerful than in the beliefs about the respective attributes of men and women. It is no accident that the characteristics assigned to men and women are precisely those required to maintain the present structure of society. It needs resourceful, competitive and dominant men to run its race just as it needs passive women who will cater to those men and stay home to care for their children.

Girls are no more naturally submissive than boys are naturally dominant. Their socialisation into these codes of behaviour is, however, based on the assumption that they *are* innate characteristics. This is the classic example of the self-fulfilling prophecy, so aptly demonstrated by Jacobsen and Rosenthal in their book 'Pygmalion in the Classroom'. The authors' experiment dealt with children in school in California. The investigators told the teachers that a group of children, taken from across the ability range, would make "intellectual spurts" in the near future. In fact, the authors had chosen

4

the children at random, but when they subsequently tested the children, it was found that this group performed substantially better than their class mates. What had happened was that the teachers had communicated their higher expectations to these children and they duly responded by improving their performance. The startling implications of this study have been largely ignored. No other social experiment has demonstrated quite so clearly that a person's ability, behaviour and self-image are dependent not on his or her genetic make-up but on the whole nexus of social expectations in which she or he is caught.

The self-fulfilling prophecy which every girl is heir to is largely negative. It goes roughly like this: you will not occupy high office (anything from a shop steward to a works manager, professor or director), you will not make scientific, medical or technical advances, you will not be a composer, train driver, engineer or inventor unless you are extraordinarily talented and determined. You will, however, place yourself at a man's disposal so that he can be any of these things. It is at this point that male sceptics, from their privileged position, when confronted with the movement for women's liberation, wail "But women must be inferior. Where are your great artists, politicians, scientists and explorers?" The nexus of psychological and cultural expectations burdens women with being all the things which men are not and burdens men with being all the things that women are not.

There has been a large and impressive amount of research done on the differences between the sexes, but the fact is that until adolescence, there are very few. In intellectual performance girls are, in fact, slightly ahead of boys and when the eleven plus examination was in existence, adjustments had to be made to bring the examination marks of boys up to the levels of girls'. What is surprising is not that these studies show that girls do indeed have all the qualities previously accorded only to boys – alertness, adventurousness, creativity and imagination – but that it takes them so long to catch on that they're not supposed to be like that. But the self-fulfilling prophecy works in devious ways. In school attainment, their intellectual capacities may emerge for a considerable time before they are gradually contained in adolescence, but long before that, girls have learnt to submit to the controls of feminity.

Carol Smith and Charles Smith summarised the mass of research which has been done on the lowered expectations and inferior self-image of school girls.

‘Numerous studies show that girls, from elementary school to college, have lower expectations of accomplishment in intellectual and academic activities than boys, even though girls typically have somewhat better grades. . . . After self-perceived failure, girls rate their ability at the task substantially lower than boys. . . . In general girls tend to downgrade their abilities.’[3]

As girls reach adolescence and as the female role closes in on them, they find it is not enough merely to lower their expectations and underestimate their abilities; they must also disguise what little they are left with. Ann Oakley reported in her book, ‘Sex, Gender and Society’:

‘One American study reported that over half a sample of 163 American college women pretended to be intellectually inferior to their boyfriends, 14% very often and 43% sometimes. An earlier study conducted elsewhere in the United States came up with comparable figures, suggesting that the habit is widespread.’[4]

A smart girl pretends she isn't. If further proof is needed of the pressure on girls to suppress their abilities in the interests of their feminine role, then consider that, at the age of sixteen, the number of boys and girls taking and passing G.C.E. 'O' Levels is fairly even. At eighteen, there are only a third as many girls taking 'A' Levels and at University boys outnumber girls by over three to one.

The process by which girls grow up to be living examples of the self-fulfilling prophecy begins in the home. Observations on the rearing practices of parents frequently show that though parents claim to treat their boy and girl children alike, deeper examination reveals great differences. Parental philosophy appears in the male and female roles being regarded as equal but different, and complementary rather than superior and inferior; where the boy is encouraged to be outward looking, the girl counters by being inward looking; where the boy may be allowed a little deviancy, the girl is encouraged to conform, and so on. This wouldn't be too bad if the male/female qualities were held in equal esteem, but as the girl rapidly discovers for herself, it's a man's world and if she wants a place in it, she must defer, flatter, please and cajole the male into accepting her into it.

The picture which emerges from the studies of girls' and boys' upbringing shows very clearly that far from things getting better, the division between the sexes is growing deeper. The influences of the toy market, television and education confirm and increase the pressure on boys and girls to pursue their separate ways at an ever earlier age. In my own local store, all children's toys and games, even those for toddlers, are divided according to sex and customers are always asked what sex of child they are buying for when they approach the toy department. The shop assistant firmly re-directed me when I went for the 'wrong' shelf. The boys' toys are mechanical, constructive and often, blatantly aggressive – cars, construction sets and weapons. The girls' toys (and there is a much smaller range of toys for girls) are exclusively oriented to the domestic world – dolls, washing machines etc. (see Toys, Books and Television).

Against this background of pressure, it is hardly surprising to discover that:

&Studies show that children's ideas of what behaviour is appropriate to each sex have hardly changed at all in recent years, contrary to what is commonly believed. Where they have changed, it tends to be in the direction of labelling *more* rather than *fewer* characteristics as appropriate for a particular sex.9[5]

The most startling evidence of the thoroughness of children's separate conditioning comes from children who have been wrongly sexed at birth – genetic and chromosomal boys who have been reared as girls and vice versa. There are many cases on record of the terrible problems these children face when they are told of the mistake. Two such cases throw a lot of light on how the behaviour and abilities of children are not determined by their biology but by their conditioning and upbringing. The first case was reported by Dr. John Money who, together with other investigators, has done a lot of work on the problem at the Endocrine Clinic at the John Hopkins Hospital in the U.S. Ann Oakley summarised one of his findings:

&A male patient reared as a female reinforces a theory to explain female under-achievement; this person first came for consultation when male secondary characteristics began to develop in adolescence (and he still thought he was female). Laboratory tests revealed maleness and the child was told of this; then followed his *social conversion* from female to male. Part of this conversion was a dramatic change in his school record. Instead of being a 'mediocre' student he became an 'excellent' one. Significantly, he began to be top of his class at mathematics, a subject in which he had done very poorly when he thought he was a girl.'[6] (my emphasis).

The problem appears more acute when the situation is reversed. Angela Hamblin, in her article '*Ultimate Goals*', recounts the case of five-year-old Frankie, a boy, who was found in hospital to have a clitoris which had previously been mistaken as a small penis. "After the diagnosis had been made, the nurses in the hospital were instructed to treat Frankie as a girl." The doctors on the case reported:

'This didn't sound too difficult – until we tried it. Frankie simply didn't give the right cues. It is amazing how much your response to a child depends on that child's behaviour towards you. It was extremely difficult to keep from responding to Frankie's typical little boy behaviour in the same way that I responded to other boys in the ward. And to treat Frankie as a girl was jarringly out of key. . . . Frankie became increasingly aware of the change in our attitude towards her. She seemed to realise that behaviour which had previously brought forth approval was no longer approved.'[7]

When Frankie's mother brought a dress to the hospital for her to go home in she "set up a howl". As Angela Hamblin points out: "*She* had not changed – it was her *sex label* that had changed."

The crux of the conditioning process is that which substitutes femininity for humanity. It is the girl's means of survival in a world dominated by men and in which femininity is her only ticket of entry. The fundamental tenets of femininity are expressed in the whole repertoire of female behaviour – the shy smile, the downward glance, the self-effacement, the apologies for one's existence, the suppressed giggle, the show of interest when a male is speaking, the hours spent in front of the mirror, the beguiling tactics, the helplessness when a male is in the vicinity and the camp follower mentality and, most crucially, the rejection of one's own sex in preference for the company of males. These are public signals which define the female as secondary and subordinate to the male.

The groundwork for this successful transition from child into girl is first laid when the baby is wrapped in a pink blanket and the mother's heart sinks just a little (especially if it's her first child) when the midwife says "It's a girl". (A friend of mine was scared to face her husband when her second baby was also a girl.) On the other hand, many women do take a secret delight in giving birth to a girl because, as one newly delivered 19-year-old girl said, "I've got her whole wardrobe planned out." Couples who want to adopt a baby also plump for girls because they are thought to be more amenable to discipline and they can be dressed up. Prospective adopting parents are now advised that, if they're really keen, they ought to consider a boy because the waiting list is so long for girls. Because femininity is an absolute quality, with identifiable limits, it can be imposed on girls regardless of their personal talents or inclination. Masculinity, on the other hand, is far more flexible, and never involves the outright objectification of its victims in the way that femininity does.

In most societies of the world, childhood is regarded as a protracted interlude, a time of preparation for adulthood and, particularly in the industrialised societies, a period of freedom from responsibility. But successful adjustment to the adult female role demands that much more emphasis be put on preparation for adulthood on girls than on boys. Wm. Goode noted that:

> 6Appropriate behaviour in a female varies as she shifts her attention from dolls to boyfriends and from her babies to her married children.9[8]

Dolls, boyfriends, babies and grandchildren – the four ages of woman! All the studies undertaken in the West on child rearing patterns show that the qualities encouraged in girls are precisely those they will need in their adult role – dependence, obedience, nurturance, and conformity while boys are encouraged to be self-reliant, active, dominant and outward-looking. Even the very youngest children, judging from the findings of researchers, are subjected to these controls. By the age of five, it has been found the great majority of children, in the psychological test situation, are spot-on in their choice of sex-typed toys, with the girls choosing toys which are wholly concerned with their domestic role and the boys choosing toys which are exclusive to the outside world.

The spectacle of so many girls fulfilling society's prophecy would be bewildering were it not for the fact that it can be viewed against this background of careful and thorough preparation. How, exactly, is it done? In the first place by trial and error. The young girl learns that approval from her parents, friends and teachers is contingent upon the degree to which she can approximate to feminine behaviour. Frankie, the little girl who had been reared as a boy, discovered that behaviour "which had always brought forth approval, was no longer approved". But in a girl, appearance can come before behaviour, for the very first requirement of a girl is that she should be pretty. Even if she isn't pretty, in the conventional sense of the word, her mother will dress her up and say "There's a pretty girl", so that by the time she can speak she has a very good idea of what pretty means and, worse, what it means *not* to be pretty.

The corollary for this is dirt. Where girls are encouraged to keep themselves neat and tidy, boys are encouraged to prove their masculinity with dirt. A TV advert for washing powder shows a young mother standing guard over her washing machine when her small dirty son enters from the garden where other boys can be seen playing war games; mother smiles lovingly to herself, thinking "Just like a boy" but Persil will solve her problems. And we know that he will continue to behave "just like a boy" and that she is doomed to send him out in a clean shirt only to wash it again the next day. A girl could never be used in such an advert, first because girls are not supposed to get that dirty and secondly because her mother could not be shown smiling to herself. Rather, the girl would be scolded for playing in the mud. Girls are shown much more frequently and to much greater effect in adverts for washing up liquid where they can be shown rehearsing their adult trade and, incidentally, caring for their hands.

Activities which are approved of in a girl, but discouraged in a boy, are not so very far from the world of adverts. The stereotype and the reality meet when the little girl spends her time playing nurse to brother's doctor, or demanding a toy sewing machine for Christmas, pushing a toy pram, trying on mother's make-up, weighing the flour for a cake or singing lullabies to her doll and refusing to join in the rough games of the boys.

A girl may refuse the constraints of femininity during the period of childhood which the psychoanalyists have called 'latency' – that is, between the ages of about seven and eleven. She may climb trees, play football, get into scrapes and generally emulate acceptable masculine behaviour, but only *on condition that she grows out of it*. No such tolerance is extended to the boy. He can never, even temporarily, abdicate from his role. The boy who goes around with girls, plays girls' games and rejects his male peers would very probably be referred to Child Guidance. Whatever perspective we take on the boy/girl polarity, it is always the boy who represents the exciting and the desirable and to experience it, the girl has to identify with the male. The traffic is only one way, for while girls can cross the boundary to enter, for a short while, the company of boys, a boy may not join ranks with his inferiors.

In the realm of physical activity there are also differing expectations of acceptable behaviour. Even within the womb and as small infants, boys are commonly supposed to be more energetic. These beliefs are founded on myth for, in terms of girls' physical development they are, age for age, slightly ahead of boys until adolescence when they level out, as a series of television programmes on the growth and development of children showed. Both their muscular development, their co-ordination and their height are in advance of boys. One of the films in the series showed a group of eight-and nine-year-old children on an adventure training course, and while the boys swung happily on a rope across a river, the girls merely sat on the bank and watched admiringly. The commentator remarked that it

13

was psychological and not physical restraint which prevented the girls from crossing the river. Already at nine years of age, girls have internalised the attitudes appropriate to their adult roles, believing and behaving as though boys are stronger, braver and more active than they are.

By the time a girl is old enough to go to school, she has learnt a good deal about the division of labour, activity and power between the sexes. She has a very good idea of what women are for and what men are for. She sees her mother working in the house all day but she knows that what her mother does is not work, because it is her father who goes out to work. Work means being out of the house all day and earning money.

"Where's Daddy gone?"
"To work."
"What for?"
"To make some money."
"Why?"
"Because everybody has to have money to buy food and clothes and things. That's why he goes to work."

The little girl of five knows an awful lot.

* * * * * * *

School

THE full impact of being female will be experienced when the little girl first starts school. It would be possible to list all the ways in which girls are treated differently from boys in our schools, but I have chosen instead to describe some ordinary experiences of a seven-year-old girl in a primary school.

At morning assembly the headmaster relates a story from the Bible about Jesus and the disciples, their saintliness and dedication. There are no women in the cast of characters. The school then says a prayer to God and calls him 'He'. The headmaster then announces that the football team scored a triumph in its match the previous afternoon and the school applauds the boys' skill.

Back in the classroom, the teacher gives the children "free choosing time" until morning break. The activities available are woodwork, painting, sewing, weaving, meccano, dressing up and Wendy House play. The girl goes for the meccano at the same time as a boy. He protests to the teacher who decides that the boy can play with it "today", but would she like to paint a picture or do some weaving? No? Well maybe she can play with the meccano when the boy has finished with it. The teacher doesn't remember but the same conversation took place the previous day with the same outcome. The girl finally adjusts to painting a picture.

At playtime, the teacher on duty allows the school ball into the playground. The boys kick it around and enjoy themselves while the girls stand about in small groups, some of them playing desultorily with a skipping rope. The ball arrives where a group of girls are standing and one of them picks it up and runs off with it, calling to the others to follow. The tough boy of the class comes up to her and demands it back. She refuses. He hits her. Other boys shout encouragement. Teacher appears and, seeing the situation, asks the girl quietly to give the ball back to the boys. She obeys. Teacher perfunctorily tells the boys that it's not nice to hit girls. The boy is triumphant and the girl is thoroughly humiliated but the teacher goes off believing that she has dealt with the situation perfectly fairly.

After break, the little girl writes her news. The only interesting thing she has done recently is visit her grandmother, so she writes about this and about the biscuits which she helped her gran to make and, tagged onto her news, she remarks that sometimes she wishes she were a boy so that she could play football. Every day the teacher reads out a piece of work and she always emphasises that it must be interesting. Today she reads out a piece by one of the football-playing boys. It is an account of how he went fishing with his elder brother and father and caught an eel. The teacher and the children are all duly impressed. When the girl shows the teacher her work, her only comment is about the neatness of the girl's writing.

The last part of the afternoon is spent on rehearsing the dramatisation of a story they heard the previous afternoon. The story is about a brave young boy who rescues a beautiful princess from a wicked witch. The boy has to perform some exacting tasks to satisfy the king that he is brave enough to attempt the job. The boy comes from a poor peasant family of six brothers, all of whom have left home to make their fortunes in the world. There are only two parts in the story for girls – the beautiful princess who has no lines and the wicked witch.

All the princess has to do is smile when she is saved and be married to the brave young man. The king is powerful and authoritative and rules over his kingdom with an iron hand. The brave boy excels in his task and brings back not only the princess but also the witch, whom the king condemns to death. The play concludes with the young couple living happily ever after.

At the end of the school day the girl walks home with her friend. They pass a small group of boys from their class playing marbles in the gutter and ask if they can play too. One of the boys agrees instantly but he is ruthlessly overruled by the others. The girls stick their tongues out at the boys, giggle to each other, but walk home somewhat dejectedly to have their tea and watch some television.

* * * * * * *

Most of these experiences will be repeated in one form or another every day of the primary school child's life (1,400 days). No girl can fail to learn the lesson. The very structure of the school is a paradigm of social values; the teachers are women, the head is a man. The school nurse who comes in every week to look at bruises, infected fingers and dirty heads is a familiar regular while the arrival of the (male) doctor once a term with stethoscope, injections and white coat is an event calling for reverence.

The daily religious service is a true reflection of male bias in the Church. In this context, the women that the children will most often hear about are Eve and Mary, who personify the two extremes of stereotyped womanhood – the sexual symbol, temptress and source of evil and Mary, the pure, silent, passive virgin-mother.

17

Several times in one day, the girl was put into a position where she had to give way to a boy's wishes. She learnt that not only do his needs take priority over her own but, as with the incidents of the football, news writing and meccano, that boys' activities are more enjoyable and more exciting than girls'. The difference between the boys' and girls' outside activities is enormous. While the girls go shopping with their mothers, the boys enjoy everything from fishing, pigeon fancying and ferreting to rugby and football.

All reading schemes in schools perpetuate this sort of division between the sexes and the seven-year-old must plough her way through book after book representing these extremes. Both the 'Janet & John' and 'Ladybird' series are very widely used in schools; they are idealised children, the sky is always blue, mother is always happy in the kitchen and father has a car and a briefcase. In both series, the brother is older, taller and probably brighter than the sister. Whenever they play out together the boy always takes the lead in their activities but mostly the boy is out helping father do something constructive while the sister is indoors helping mother in the kitchen. One typical illustration in the Ladybird series shows a boy half way up a tree, proudly looking down on his sister, while she stands feebly watching him. In the Janet & John series the two characters are by a harbour and John says "Look Janet". She's too dumb to see for herself.

A study done in America of 134 books published by 14 major publishing companies involving 2,760 stories for elementary school children found the house-wife-mother figure presented as a:

'. . . limited, colourless, mindless creature . . . Not only does she wash, cook, clean, nurse and find mittens; these chores constitute her only happiness.

In illustration, she frequently appears in the servant's posture, body slightly bent forward, hands clasped, eyes riveted on the master of the house or the children.'[1]

Perhaps the most influential model that is brought to bear on children is contained in the fairy stories and adventure stories told and read in schools. The basic plot of the great majority of stories for young primary school children is the same as the one which the children dramatised. The hero is almost always a boy, quite often from a poor but honest background, who makes good in the world and usually gets to marry a princess or the daughter of a rich landowner. She, of course, is never consulted on her wishes but is a prize for the boy's bravery and strength. The obverse of this is the Cinderella story, which is doubly pernicious in that it offers marriage into a higher social class as a girl's only reason for living. The benign witch in Cinderella is a rare figure. The classic witch, as a personification of evil, crops up in most stories. Hansel and Gretel is one well known example. Occasionally, the witch is dispensed with, only to reappear in the guise of a wicked stepmother. Traditionally, her power has to be overcome by a brave and resourceful young man, a symbol of strength and right. Other variations of the same theme are the many stories where the wicked witch is set against the benign Wizard ('The Tales of Arthur' is one example), who puts his magical powers to good use. I have never, in five years of infant school teaching, succeeded in finding a story where these traditional male/female roles are reversed – where a woman represents a force for good and where the man represents a force for evil. Similarly, there are no stories in which a brave young girl rescues a kidnapped prince or where there are good stepmothers and bad

19

fathers or where the girl refuses to be carried off by prince charming on his white charger. Teachers always find it interesting that when it comes to dramatising these stories, the girls are always eager to play the witch/stepmother figure, rather than the good but anaemic role of the princess. But the witch character does offer the opportunity to take an active and instrumental part in the proceedings, unlike the princess who merely has to *be*.

As children move on up the school, these kinds of stories give way to tales of mystery and adventure and 'true' accounts of intrepid explorers, inventive scientists, warlike generals, wise statesmen, crusading Kings and so on. The models that are first posed in the younger stories are vigorously reinforced, except that the female figure recedes more and more until she fades right out of the picture. The only exception to this is in the books which are written exclusively for girls, which no boy would be caught dead reading and which no teacher would use as a basis for classroom activity. In some of the stories, the girls do very adventurous things, but these books are intended for private consumption and, unlike the parade of men's glorious history which all girls must accept as facts in school, these books are clearly in the fantasy bracket. In any case, they tend to be very old-fashioned and deal with upper class girls in private boarding schools who lose their ponies.

No girl or boy can get through school without learning about Florence Nightingale. She will, very likely, be the only female figure in a long cast of famous, important people whom school children learn about. History, as it is taught in schools, is very definitely the history of *men*. Josephine Butler, Sylvia Pankhurst, Mary Wollstencraft and the many neglected women who were instrumental both in the Middle Ages and in the Industrial Revolution are all consigned to historical oblivion. But Florence Nightingale is singled out for special mention. The fact that she was a very radical woman (in fact, one of many) who broke social conventions is ignored. Her fame rests as a nurse, a symbol of female virtue. It is interesting to speculate why it is, that of all the radical women and men of the 19th century, she has been elevated until she is now nothing more than a cardboard figure on which teachers and text book writers can pin their prejudices. Stories of female missionaries are also made much of in the later years of primary school and their impact on children must not be underestimated. By the time they are ten or eleven most girls are conscious of deep frustration in their allotted role, and the missionary-nurse figure, whom they are asked to identify with, represents, on one level, the ideal of nurturance and goodness which is their female province and, on another level, the ideal holds the promise of positive *activity*. There are very few girls who survive their school days without at some point wishing to be either a nurse or a missionary. (It should be stated here that schools have traditionally regarded missionaries in the same light as saints; they are sacrosanct. The value of breaking up non-industrial societies in the name of the gospel goes unquestioned.)

The degree to which the school succeeds in imposing on boys and girls their respective roles in society can be gauged by the following pieces of written work produced by school children in a working class area in the North of England. The subject was "Why I like/ don't like being a boy/girl". The children were also asked to imagine that they were of the opposite sex.

Paul Linley. Age 11.
I would not like to be a girl because I cannot play foot-

ball or cricket or play with my bogey. I would not be able to play with my friends because I would have to wash up. If I was a girl I would not like to do the house because I would be tired of working in the house with the others sat down. I would be jealous of the others. I am glad I'm not a girl. I'm a boy.

Gaynor Wood. Age 10.

I think the wives should stop at home and do the house-work because if the man does it it will not look as nice as if the wife did. I would not like to be a boy because they are always having fights and they are always getting told off. When I am older I would like to have a job in a vets looking after all animals and helping them to get better from their illness and when I get home to get the tea ready for the children and their dad. I would like to be a vet so if my dog or cat got ill I could help it.

Abdul Patel. Age 11.

I would not like to be a girl because girls are not strong and they do not know how to fight. Boys chase them. They cannot do anything about it. If they do anything wrong to the girls they will hit them and when they grow up they have babies and homework [sic] to do. They do not get any money out of that but men go to work and get money.

Women go to work. They sew some clothes and needles go in their fingers and they have to pick up clothes and that is hard for women because they are not strong.

Karen Douglas. Age 11.

I would like to be a boy then they can't stop me from playing football and then we men can drink beer and shandy and we will be stronger than them. They [women] will have to do harder jobs than us. They will have to get the baby ready, the dinner ready, they will have to make the beds and sweep up the floor and tidy the kitchen.

Stephen Schofield. Age 10.

If I was a girl I would work in a supermarket and a dressmaker. I would not like to be a girl because you have to do the washing up and clean the house and you couldn't play football or rugby so I would not like to be a girl. A girl hasn't got patience to do jigsaws or anything else so I would not like to be a girl. Girls are soft and weak and they haven't got the brains to play rugby or football.

Usha Patel. Age 10.

I think the wives should do all the housework and doing the cleaning up. Some of the wives go out to work and then the husbands have to do the work.

Susan Lockwood. Age 11.

When I get married I would like to have a maid to do the work and me and my husband would go out to work and we would have about £50 coming in the house. I would pay the maid £10 and she could live with us and we would have a house off in the country. How nice it would be.

Walter Pawinski. Age 10.

A job that a girl can do is a teacher. And girls should do the housework and a very good job for a girl is nurse and cleaning. A good job for a boy is policeman and fireman. I would not like to be a girl because of the things they do and the clothes they wear.

Asha Patel. Age 11.

I would not like to be a boy because they are mucky and they play a lot of mucky games and they play in dirty water and make their legs dirty.

Susan Wallace. Age 9.
I like being a girl because I like to push a pram and do handstands and play with my doll.

Stephen Bland. Age 10.
Women's jobs are washing dishes and doing all the cleaning and washing the table and the banister and watering the flowers and doing everything in the house. I would not like to be a girl because they wear ribbons and dresses and high heel shoes.

These children's attitude to appropriate behaviour for boys and girls and their expectations of adult life are as accurate as they are rigid. Well meaning educationalists, broadcasting pundits and newspaper columnists talk confidently about the changing roles of men and women; they point to the improved career opportunities for women and the 'permissive' society as evidence for the equality of women, as though this were a reality for the great mass of people instead of an illusion for the privileged few.

These children's identification with their sex roles was well formed before they were five years old. The experience of school only serves to confirm and reinforce them. Despite the move towards progressive and liberal teaching methods in primary schools, the question of the treatment of girls remains a non-starter. Some educationalists may talk of the 'blurring of the sex roles' but these views have not yet penetrated the schools.

Attitudes to sex roles are as entrenched in the colleges of education as they are in the schools themselves. The emphasis, even in the most liberal of institutions, is always on exploiting the child's 'natural' and innate abilities. In practice, the innate abilities of children are assumed to correspond exactly to the abilities they will need as adults. In the classroom, this turns out to be preparatory work for adulthood and in the infant class, where the pattern for their entire school lives is first laid down, girls are pushed to express themselves in domestic play in the Wendy House while the boys practise their mechanical skills with the bricks. Even in those schools which pride themselves on their progressive methods, girls will still be found fulfilling their conventional tasks – washing up the teachers' cups, serving at table, sewing, cooking and caring for the younger children. Sport, of course, continues to be severely segregated in both primary and secondary schools, with all the prestige activities assigned to the boys.

But certainly, there are schools in which token attempts to 'blur the sex roles' are being made; girls will be allowed to do woodwork and the boys may be encouraged to take their turn at cookery, but by the time these children reach secondary school, outside pressures to conform to appropriate behaviour weigh very much more heavily. The boy of eight who happily slopped flour about the classroom is a very different sight from the boy of thirteen who, fearful for his masculinity, resists any activity which might be labelled 'cissy'. Whatever steps schools may take towards equality of treatment for boys and girls, they cannot hope to counteract the pressures of the outside society. They may succeed, occasionally, in presenting the *possibility* of alternative patterns of behaviour, but these can never become a reality while external pressures remain so entrenched and inevitable.

The hopelessness of the situation in education can be illustrated by the following extract from the Newsome Report on Secondary Education:

‘The main groups of occupations most widely taken up by girls – jobs in offices, in shops, in catering, work in the clothing industry and other manufacturing trades – can all provide the material for courses at more than one level of ability. For all girls too, there is a group of interests relating to what many, perhaps most of them, would regard as their most important vocational concern, marriage. It is true that at the age of 14 or 15 this may appear chiefly as preoccupation with personal appearance and boyfriends, but many girls are ready to respond to work relating to the wider aspect of homemaking and family life and upbringing of children.’[2]

In other words this is how it is, so let's set about keeping it like that. Most of the boys will expect to be married too, one supposes, and have children, but Newsome says nothing about preparing them for their "most important vocational concern".

It is precisely because marriage and motherhood are presented as girls' only vocation – their whole life and career – that girls are taught in school to regard their work and their education as a necessary but, in the long run, wasteful exercise. This is no less true for those girls who are labelled 'successes'. University is a possibility for only a very tiny minority. By far the largest number of sixth form girls are channelled into teacher training and for one very obvious reason. It is held out as a steady job which can easily be fitted in with their primary role in life, marriage and motherhood. They can take a few years off to have their babies and then return to teaching. The hours and the holidays make it possible to combine their triple role – housewife, mother and teacher. So off they dutifully trot, packing out the colleges of education

26

with a ratio of over three women to one man – the only profession in which women outnumber men.

A friend of mine who describes herself as 'plain' tells the following true story. She queued up to see her careers master (in a co-ed school) in the first year sixth, along with all the other girls in her year. They were all going to take three 'A' levels. Each girl was told that she was bound to get married and the best thing to do would be to apply for a teacher training course. When it came to her, he spouted the same thing and then, taking a second look at her, said, "Well, perhaps not. Perhaps you ought to try for University."

These attitudes which prevail in schools, Universities and colleges of education are precisely those expressed in the Newsome Report. So long as everyone in education is locked in a network of expectations about the respective roles of men and women, any hope that education will pave the way for a more humane future is in vain.

* * * * * * *

Toys, Books and Television

TOYS which mirror the life style of the grown ups are now big business. For small boys, this is manifested in toy guns, rockets, cars, aeroplanes and hovercrafts, though exactly whose life style the boys are supposed to be emulating is hard to fathom. Perhaps, like their fathers, they are being taught to compensate for the dreariness of their work-lives by fantasising about exciting alternatives. The situation is very different for girls. Here, the toys are exact replicas of the everyday tools of their mothers' trade. Rehearsing their adult role is a much more serious business for girls than it is for boys. Girls may not dream of a life of excitement, adventure and travel away from home, husband and family. If any fantasy is allowed in their play with toys it is tightly controlled by the reality. They can dream of the *kind* of home they will have and *who* they will marry. To this end the market is flooded with every conceivable kind of domestic toy, from dolls to miniature baking tins. Even neutral playthings are not immune. On the cover of a pack of interlocking bricks the girl is shown how to assemble a sewing machine while the boy is shown a gun. A reporter from the *Sunday Times* was told at the British & International Toy Fair held in Brighton on Jan. 29th 1972 that "painstaking research has revealed that the new target for toymakers is the mother-to-be of the mid eighties".[1] The exploitation of little girls with their 'demand' for expensive toy prams, pushchairs, dolls and cradles, cookers, washing machines and even washing lines and pegs, toy hoovers, dustpans and tea sets has brought every manufacturer in the business to her immediate service. Raleighs, the cycle manufacturers, have recently jumped onto the bandwagon and have brought out seven new models with prices up to £20 for a *toy* pram. According to their research, their readiest market is to be found amongst the working class. One of the biggest (and most expensive) sellers in dolls is 'Tracey' who "pours out tea and offers cakes with her big blue eyes glancing up and down as she serves her guests".

The *Guardian* reported that the competition for the lucrative doll market had hotted up for the 1973 Brighton Toy Fair. Small dolls (though the word 'doll' is never used) are now made for boys, under such names as 'Action Man' and 'Little Big Man', which are sold with action packed accessories for the boys to fantasise with – snow shoes, ropes, kit bags and three adventure themes – and all of them include miniature weapons. An exciting and violent vision of the outdoor life. And for girls? The new dolls are precocious. Their outfits are designed by Mary Quant with pants and boots; 24 outfits for each doll selling at around 60–90p. each. The dolls themselves are described as "music loving, record crazy teenagers with the latest trendy fashion clothes".[2] The vision of excitement for girls is short lived. It comes full circle through the discotheque back into the kitchen; for the other side of the doll market for girls is the enormous range of baby dolls "which cry and need a dummy or shoulder patting to stop the noise". Nothing in the toy market for girls deviates from the twin ideals they are being taught to aspire to; for these dolls symbolise the twin stereotypes of femininity – the sex object, flashing and alluring, which leads inexorably to the mother figure. And both stereotypes deny a girl personhood – she is never herself but merely someone's girl friend, then someone's wife and then someone else's mother.

Less deliberate but just as effective as the toy market is the influence of television in shaping children's self image. But where the toy manufacturers go to great lengths with their research to woo the custom of little girls (and their parents), television planners seem not to be aware of girls' existence. Between the hours of 4 p.m. and 9 p.m. (and children watch, on average, an hour and a half of television every day), nine times as many men as women appear on the screen. The differential is slightly less on the commercial channel because women predominate, as housewives, in the advertisements. I believe that this overwhelming under-representation of women does more to perpetuate the division between the sexes than the actual way in which women are presented.

In the programmes specifically for children, men outnumber the women by about three to one. The usual format is to have a woman presenter who merely announces the proceedings, followed by men who *initiate* them. More male biased than these are the cartoons. The characters, whether ingenious mouse, aggressive cat, free-wheeling duck or flying superman are all male. On the rare occasions when a female appears in the animal cartoons, the music changes and becomes seductive, the drums hum and on wiggles a curvy mouse with knee length boots and long eyelashes. The parallel with her human counterpart is glaringly obvious. Girls as desirable objects are O.K. *in their place,* but on no account can they be admitted as equals into male company; nor can they participate in the action. Or else the female appears in the guise of her other human stereotype, the mother figure. The mark of her feminity is not long eyelashes and seductive ways but an apron and bonnet. With some rare exceptions, these are the only ways in which the female half of humanity is ever presented in cartoons – long eyelashes or aprons. It is no wonder that, after watching ten years of television, girls get the impression that they are a minority group, instead of 51% of the population.

Story telling takes a great slice of children's television. In a month of viewing children's TV programmes I came up with this ratio – for every four stories featuring a boy, there was one which featured a girl. One typical story, beautifully told and illustrated, was shown on Jackanory.[3] The story featured the standard brave, resourceful boy who outwitted his uncle and was carried off to the land of the eagle people, the chief of whom had two daughters. Our hero, who carried on with his brave duties and flew about in an eagle costume, was offered the choice of either of these girls as a bride. The only point to their presence in the story was to show the girls arguing which one would have the boy for a husband and he, naturally, chose 'the prettier' of the two. End of story. How inconceivable, after a diet of this kind of stuff, for girls ever to imagine a story in which they are brave and self reliant and resourceful and are offered the choice of a passive, onlooking husband?

If the children's programmes are so heavy with male bias then the adults' programmes are a thousand times worse. (Many of the children I taught watched television every night until 9.30 or 10 during the winter evenings.) Apart from the gross numerical under-representation of women, children also come face to face with television's dominant image of woman as someone who doesn't *work*. Men are portrayed, whether in the news, the adverts, the plays or the regular series, in *occupations*, whether as a policeman, news reader, problem solver, muck-raker, doctor, lawyer, detective, star ship commander, soldier, comedian, pop star, politician, salesman, business executive, train driver, pilot and expert on everything from animal design to pollution.

Although there are women in most of these fields, the only occupations in which they are presented are servicing ones – dishwashers, waitresses, cleaners, and secretaries to the businessmen and nurse to the doctors. (Imagine a soap opera hospital series where John, nurse at Oxbridge County Hospital, falls in love with Jane, doctor!)

Tabulating the roles in which women appear results in this – the idle wife lounging on a settee in the glossy play; the adoring, mindless mother in the advert worrying about the whiteness of her wash; the leg-kicking chorus girl; the down trodden prisoner's wife in Z Cars, Softly Softly etc.; the giggling contorting dancer in Top of the Pops; the deodorising 'dolly' girl in the advert; the jealous wife in 'Public Eye'; the devoted wife waiting at home for her explorer/prisoner of war husband in the news; the boardroom secretary who says 'Yes Sir' and overruling it all, the beauty image, characterised by the token women used in such series as Mission Impossible and Startrek. The only escape route from all this is the female pop star or folk singer, though again, women in the pop field are outnumbered by men by about 20 to 1.

The dominant image of woman as nothing more than a devoted foil to men, whether as a human symbol for sex or as a dish-washer, has a profound effect on children. Both boys and girls, whatever their home lives are like, grow up believing that women only come in two models – the dolly girl and the full time mother/housewife. And girls, especially, have to believe that they will be the dolly girl *in order to be* the full time mother. And if they fail to learn that lesson, then they will still end up with the view of women as funny/dirty subjects for jokes. Dick Emery and the Monty Python team appear to believe that the fact of womanhood is, itself, comic, and when they're stuck for getting a laugh, they merely dress up as women and affect high voices so that the whole audience rolls about in their seats. They don't reverse the procedure because there's nothing funny about the oppressed imitating the oppressor. But worse than this is the Morecambe and Wise nudge in the ribs, or the Dave Allen snigger at femaleness; for their jokes do not hinge on sex but on *women*; there are about three or four such jokes every night on television. One typical one was told by Dick Emery: "Racquel Welch joined women's liberation and took her bra off and everybody in the vicinity got knocked out." Peals of laughter. It isn't Racquel Welch who is funny, but *breasts*.

Many older girls, midway in a process of growing up and clinging on to their view of themselves as different, turn to fiction for solace and confirmation of themselves as human beings. But if they want to read about mystery, fantasy and adventure, they are asked, yet again, to identify with the standard all-purpose boy hero, for the girls in these stories are distorted travesties of what a girl is, feels herself to be and can do. Like her animated female counterpart in the cartoon, girls are a *nuisance*. She interferes with the action and breaks an ankle on the trail and if it were not for the inventive genius of the boy hero in finding a new clue, the story would have to come to a grinding halt. Occasionally girls are allowed a place in mystery/adventure fiction provided they abandon their girlness and become pseudo boys (e.g. George in 'Famous Five').

Only about one children's book in ten has a girl as a central character. Often they are lonely, solitary and bookish girls who have retreated from the contradictions of femininity into a world of their own making. Predictably, they are brought out of solitude by romance and the promise of future marriage and happiness. As if to satisfy girls' yearning for solutions to their inferior self-image, there is a genre of children's fiction (though it is dying) portraying very forthright girls who do rebel against femininity. The substance of these books (e.g. 'Edie on the Warpath') revolves around the school's and family's attempts to tame the heroine back into her role which is, in itself, supposed to be *funny*. There are very few books where girls and boys are not set against each other and none at all where they are given equal weight and responsibility for carrying the plot.

Children's comics and magazines carry the stereotyped image of femaleness to its logical extreme. There are over a dozen girls' comics, with titles like 'Mandy', 'Judy', 'Jackie' and 'Melanie' competing for this profitable market. Their stock in trade is obsessional male hero worship; coloured pin-ups of Donny Osmond, David Cassidy or whoever, punctuated with accounts of the minutiae of their daily lives, competitions for the readers to enter, promising tickets to see their heroes perform live, and homilies on how to be 'the ideal girl' – decorative, adoring and silent. To counter the over-exposure of the male, editors of these comics for adolescent girls concede the occasional reality of the female identity with strip cartoons featuring Cindy, swinging fashion model, or Judy, flirtatious secretary to dashing, eligible song writer. The actuality of the readers' lives makes its agonised appearance in the problem page where the whole gamut of desirable female preoccupation is paraded – spots, jealousy, sister rivalry, unpermissive parents, wallflowerdom and unrequited romantic love – the defining limits which the media sets on adolescent female experience.

The largest advertisement in 'Melanie', the latest of the crop of comics for this age group, is a full page colour illustration of 40 or so sparkling engagement rings. The editor of the comic, when asked by Kenneth Allsop in a TV interview, why a comic for the 12-to 15-year-old girl should advertise engagement rings replied that "getting married is what young girls dream about". And if they don't, then 'Melanie' will give them a hefty nudge to make sure they do.

The comics for the pre-adolescent girl, 'Bunty', 'Tammy', 'Mandy', 'Sandie', 'June' and 'Judy', are childish preparations and rehearsals for their adolescent and, ultimately, adult role. But unlike the comics for the adolescent girls, the male is largely absent. In their all female world – ballet school, private boarding school, riding school etc. – men appear only fleetingly as fathers, policemen or chauffeurs. In place of the blatant male hero worship come the earlier conflicts in the female role which each girl has to work through. These conflicts are symbolically played out by 'Scatty Matty' ('Bunty'), 'Bessie Bunter' ('June & Pixie'), 'Dottie's Diary' ('Judy') and 'Mighty Mo' ('Bunty') who, as their names suggest, are anything but desirable models of femininity. Unlike their male counterparts in boys' comics – Dennis the Menace, Desperate Dan – they are not to be laughed with but *at*. Their ineptitude and gracelessness is a comic warning of the fate of girls who cannot or will not capitulate to femininity. And within this tight context, rivalry between girls and jostling for top place in the femininity stakes are recurring themes, so emphasised as to persuade girls that deceit and competition are necessary and even desirable aspects of the female role. But the girl who is *too* pretty and *too* feminine is already suspect:

‘Mary Coates and Angela Palmer are new girls at Charleton School. Angela has the sweetest, most angelic face but she only turns on the charm to get her own way, for underneath she's totally selfish. Now Angela has turned all the girls against Mary. . . .’[4]

Angela is a myth maker – the childish counterpart of the adult woman whose beauty spells everyone else's downfall and eventually her own. She schemes, manipulates, turns on her charms, breaks up friendships and is never to be trusted. In adult life, she is the man's woman who is contemptuous of her own sex while she charms her way into any man's heart, only to drop him like a wet fish when he's served his purpose. And the young girls who read these stories are being given a straight either/or choice. Be friendly, ordinary and passive, like the martyred Mary, or be extraordinary, charming but, necessarily, spiteful, like Angela. The moral, neatly contained in many of these comic-strip stories, is that the Marys of the world may often suffer at the hands of the Angelas, but their passivity will eventually pay off when the inevitable handsome young man comes to carry them off. But no such fate awaits the Angelas. They must pay the price of their audacity and charm, in pain and ultimate rejection.

Cresy Cannon studied the comics for young girls and in an article in the magazine *Spare Rib*, noted:

‘. . . over and over again, on both the serious and the humorous levels, the feminine role is in itself sufficiently problematic to provide the basis for most of the material in this range of comics. Their very success indicates the extent to which girls find them meaningful. In this respect girls' comics differ fundamentally from boys', for they are more than just feminine

37

versions of adventure stories, they are basically concerned with femininity itself.

A typical plot is about a girl with a talent for sport or ballet which she is forced to renounce because of family problems, and who has to take the role of mother to her younger brothers and sisters. A sort of vicarious rehearsal for the future.❜[5]

But glamorous job fantasies, family conflicts, premature maternity and diluted adventure fade into insignificance with the onslaught of romance. The whole comic market for girls is finally summed up by "The Two Sues: They talk about everything, but their favourite subject is boys!" ('Fabulous') *Everything*? Well, not quite. They talk about clothes, spots, dimples, boys, make-up, clothes, boys, dates and hair. The blonde Sue thinks her feet are too big and remarks "Chinese mothers bound their children's feet to make them tiny". Dark-haired Sue replies "What a pity your mother didn't do that for you" and she muses, as she files her nails, "We're too soft nowadays. We haven't the courage to suffer for beauty."

Timidity and romance hold hands, inseparable and each unthinkable without the other. The girl who reads her way through the comics will need more than the courage it takes to 'suffer for beauty'. She needs the courage to live with the self-contempt which streamlines her path from pink ribbons to wrinkles. S.G. of Gainsborough who wrote the following letter to 'Fabulous' is beginning to learn to live with it:

❛I am very self conscious about my thin legs. I feel I can't go out because boys laugh at me and even my best friend mocks me. I've eaten more and had tablets but nothing helps.❜[6]

S.G. would probably willingly undergo surgery to have shapely legs, but what she hasn't got and what the comics and society cannot give back to her is that which it first took away – the courage to be *human* and, in her case, merely the courage to live with thin legs.

* * * * * * *

Careering into Marriage

Alternatives to Career Marriage

A British Women's Liberation group in the South of England has revived an issue long thought dead and buried. "Marriage," they say, "is a relationship, not a career." It is a thin voice struggling to be heard against a background of propaganda which exhorts women to turn their backs on the world and devote their lives to men and children. Men are spared this. They are not bombarded with media nonsense telling them that their only purpose in life is husbandhood and fatherhood. They are not called 'old maids' if they don't marry. They are not made to feel that climbing the career ladder is a symptom of inadequacy. There are no multi-million pound industries feeding off their faces, their hair, their smell and their clothes so that they can improve their chances in the race to find a wife. There are not upwards of fifty magazines competing with each other in a market which is openly dedicated to their need to find a wife, make a home for her, cook her meals, knit her clothes and care for her children.

The bachelor's counterpart is a spinster. The word is so horrific that single women have to opt for male terminology – a bachelor girl! By avoiding the connotations of the word 'spinster', the single woman can, temporarily at least, reap some of the rewards that the term 'bachelor' suggests. But unlike the man, her time is short. She pretty soon reaches her peak, with only a long decline into spinsterhood ahead of her – a fate, apparently, worse than death. Mrs. Benson, an architect interviewed by Rhona and Robert Rapoport said "she would have died if she hadn't married".[1]

With few socially acceptable pursuits, which are not centred on her traditional domestic role, to occupy

43

her time, what options are there for the single woman other than concentrating on snaring a man? Work? A career? The prospects of finding satisfaction at work for the great majority of women is exceedingly dismal. Well over half the female work-force in this country is employed in semi-skilled and unskilled labour. And while the proportion of women employed in unskilled, menial work is rising, the proportion of men in this lowest sector is declining. The vast majority of these women work at jobs which are direct extensions of their traditional servicing role. The manufacture of food and clothing – work that was once done in the home in family-based industry – is now done in the factory and canteen for other people's profit. Overwhelmingly, women work as cleaners, packers in the food industry, in the textile industries, as waitresses and as shop assistants. A similar pattern emerges in the skilled occupations. Four times as many boys as girls receive apprenticeships, and of the girls, a staggering 97% are training to be hairdressers.

But what about the career woman? Women have been emancipated for fifty years. No woman is forced to marry. There are plenty of careers open to women. And so on. In the first place, careers are only available to a small and privileged section of women, the educated middle class. In the second, they are severely restricted in their choice of work because opportunities for girls are viewed as mere staging posts on their traditional road to marriage – nursing, teaching and office work. But despite the large majority of women in these occupations, most of the senior positions in them are held by men. Even in nursing, where one would expect discrimination against *men*, the recent influx of male nurses into the ranks has resulted in their rapid promotion, so that they now occupy many more of the responsible posts than their numbers would justify. Exactly the same pattern is apparent in education. Despite the fact that women comprise three-quarters of the total of primary school teachers, nearly two-thirds of the head-ships are held by men. Which leaves office work as just about the last refuge for the career minded woman. Again, a woman's usual place in an office is the traditional one – as a secretary. Like her counterpart in the home, the housewife, her job is to cater to all the man's needs, do his dirty work, attend to all the routine tasks which are beneath his dignity, cover up his mistakes and massage his ego. The numbers of graduate and highly qualified women who search the women's appointments column for responsible jobs, only to be asked at their interviews "Can you type?" and who finish up as glorified but disillusioned filing clerks servicing incompetent, domineering men, are legion. One way out of the situation – and many women take it – is marrying the boss. Thus the secretary reverts to the conventional road towards personal fulfilment. Instead of being a lawyer, engineer, doctor or whatever, she marries one.

Are there any career opportunities for women which are not tinged with the cloak of selfless sainthood or menial lackeydom? Medicine is perhaps the only field which can be seriously considered, yet discrimination against women in the profession is almost as rampant now as it was when Elizabeth Garrett Anderson first fought for recognition in the B.M.A., a hundred years ago. The numbers of places in medical schools available to women, regardless of the numbers applying, varies from between ten and twenty-five per cent. Once inside the medical school, the women will find themselves being urged to concentrate on exactly those specialities which reflect their role within the family – obstetrics, geriatrics and gynaecology. With heart and brain surgery topping the medical pops, it is no accident that the female specialities occupy the lowest rung, just as it is no accident that men hold the majority of the consultancies in these fields.

If she manages to push through the wall of prejudice and discrimination, the professional woman may find that she has to satisfy far more exacting standards than a man in the same position. And because there is so much resistance among men to taking orders from a woman, she has to walk an impossible tightrope between the demands of her job and the demands of 'femininity'. The mythology is such that no woman can retain her femininity while she is man's equal.

Nicholas Hoffman remarked in an excellent article on 'Man's Inhumanity to Woman':

> ... in most offices a woman in a professional position must be on time while her male counterpart can saunter in late and take two and a half hours for lunch. Men always have important things to do: women never.[2]

Christine Eade is one of the few women journalists who has not been bought off by the woman's page. She is a parliamentary lobby correspondent and she has to describe herself and behave "as one of the chaps".[3] Like her childish counterpart, the tomboy, she has to become a pseudo male before she's given entrance into a male world.

If the career woman is married with a family, she is especially vulnerable to suspicions and accusations. The demands of a career are commonly supposed to conflict with those of a family. She may be a success in her job but she's failed at the one which counts. Dodging accusations of this sort is hard work and it is no wonder that, to avoid being neatly packaged away under the label 'career woman', the woman who happens, like a man, to be committed to her work as well as to her private relationships, has to bend over backwards to prove to the world that she is first and foremost not herself, but her husband's wife and her children's mother. She is the stuff that society's ideal women are made of. She has an interesting job on the side with all the benefits of extra money and fruitful contact with the outside world, she keeps herself smart and bright, is abreast of world affairs, works hard at keeping her marriage alive and well, takes care to defer to her husband on large issues, stays off work when her children are ill, takes full responsibility for their care and the running of the home, graciously accepts her husband's 'help' and although she does three jobs – worker, housewife and mother, she never complains. The demands put on these women are intolerable. We have a society which is littered with the fragmented remains of women who have given up the struggle and have yielded to society's pressures, to conform to the normal family pattern.

For the great majority of women for whom a career is, by virtue of their class and education, out of the question, what alternatives are there other than gearing their whole lives towards marriage and motherhood which, in practice, means seeing their futures in terms of stop-gap jobs, preoccupations first with clothes and make up, then with child care and home care and then twenty or thirty more years of boring work – a life pattern which is depressingly similar for the vast majority of women in this society.

Most men and a few women would probably

argue that the barriers to women's self-realisation are of their own making, that 'it's all in the mind' and that women are free to live a full and satisfying life in this society, regardless of marriage. Such notions are based on the assumption that women have been 'emancipated' and all that they need to make use of it is determination. Their mass refusal even to attempt to break down the barriers is taken as proof of women's fundamental incapacity. The variations on this theme are endless and women have been compelled to listen to them for so long that they almost believe them. But no credit is ever given to women for rejecting emancipation if all it means is becoming 'one of the chaps' in a competitive, de-humanised male world on male terms.

Behind the discrimination against women, their inferior education and their lowered expectations lies the economic reality. It is here that any talk of equal opportunities for women and emancipation is revealed for the nonsense it is. The average weekly pay for women, in both manual and professional work is *less than half of a man's*.[4] The much touted Equal Pay Act will do virtually nothing to alter this state of affairs, because the great majority of women work at occupations which are specifically female, where there is no man with whom their pay might be equal. In those few industries where women work alongside men (notably in light engineering), employers are already busily creating special categories of 'light' work and 'heavy' work so that they will not have to implement the Equal Pay Act. Employers' associations have circulated guidance to their members on how best to evade the Act, suggesting for instance:

‘Where job evaluation is . . . used it may be possible to minimise the impact of equal pay by changing the work content of some jobs significantly so that re-

48

evaluation is justified. Alternatively, the withdrawal of men or women from certain jobs in the existing job structure may limit the scope for parity claims.'[5]

They also recommend:

'In particular, the domestic male unskilled rate must be kept as low as possible to avoid unnecessarily increasing the costs of equal pay.'[6]

The *Sunday Times*, in reporting the "secret memos" racket, noted that:

'A recent survey by the Department of Employment's Office of Manpower Economics showed that only a fifth of the companies examined had either removed or entered into a commitment to end discriminatory pay scales.'[7]

And that is three years after the Act was passed and less than two years before it is supposed to be fully implemented. But the last word on employers' self interest in withholding equal pay for women must be left to the British Paper Box Federation, an industry of 26,000 employees, seventy percent of whom are women. Their memorandum recommends:

'Fundamentally, the women's rate should become, at an agreed date, the *minimum rate* for each industry.'[8]

Even in those few occupations which, nominally at least, have achieved equal pay – teaching, civil service, the law and accountancy – the discrimination against women, the blocking of their promotion prospects which is an integral part of their functioning, has resulted in women actually receiving only between one half and two thirds of the men's average pay.

Pay structures for women are defended on the grounds that women are supported by men. It is precisely because women cannot maintain a home and a decent standard of living on their unequal pay that they have to depend on men. But what of the many thousands of women who are struggling to support aged parents (there are over 300,000 such single women) and widows, and what of the impossible struggle of women working to support their children on their single, unequal wage?[9] Must *all* women be victimised because a few, a very few, whose husbands are in the £3,000 a year bracket, need not go out to work? Just who is it who decrees that men shall be paid twice as much as women? Do women only need half as much food, clothing, housing, furniture, warmth and holidays as men?

It has been calculated that to achieve effective equal pay for women over £600 million would have to be spent. But whereas access to free education and health services is taken to be an inalienable human right, equal pay for women is not. The Government and the Confederation of British Industries and the Trade Unions, whose record on equal pay is appalling, all agree that the cost, both in financial terms and in terms of loss of male privilege, is too high a price.

Economically, socially and psychologically, all the cards are stacked against women. Men know this and women experience it. The only escape clause in the contract is marriage, and it is in this way that marriage is elevated from being a relationship between two independent people to a career for one of them. All the surveys of the respective aspirations of boys and girls bear this out. One typical study, summarised by Charles Smith and Carol Smith in *New Society*[10] reported that adolescent girls have vocational aspirations, not for themselves but for their future husbands. Rhona and Robert Rapoport, investigating the expectations of 581 sixth form girls found that "one fifth of the girls thought they would like to be full time housewives by the time they were middle aged, 66% said that ideally they would like to combine a career with marriage. Only 2% were willing to put a career before marriage". Alice Rossi, in her study of American graduate women, found a similar pattern with 20% classified as "homemakers", 50% as "traditionals", looking for a synthesis between career and family and 7% as "pioneers", prepared to put their careers at the centre of their lives. Why are boys not asked whether they would put a career before marriage? And why, anyway, should combining a career with marriage pose problems for girls but not for boys? It is always unquestioningly assumed that whether women work or not, they will take full responsibility for housework and child care, thus sparing men from having to make any choice between career or family.

As long as marriage and a family continue to be presented as women's raison d'etre and men's weekend retreat, there will be no chance of re-directing the sign-posts and turning previously sealed-off cul-de-sacs into wide open spaces, where men and women can be whole people instead of exploited workers and dishwashers.

* * * * * * *

Identity

W HERE is the young girl going to find her husband? How soon will she marry him? According to Geoffrey Gorer's large scale study on marriage, the most likely place to find a man is at the local dance hall. The length of time between meeting and getting engaged varies with social class, being shorter in the working class but altogether averaging under two years. Gorer found that nearly three times as many women as men are married before they are twenty-one years old. The men, on average, are three or four years older than their wives, and at the age of thirty, there are three times as many men marrying than women. Apart from the local dance hall, Gorer found that husbands and wives most frequently first met each other amongst only a small range of social contacts – through work, family contacts, pubs and public amusement places. The pattern that emerges from Gorer's findings is that the girl, marrying so much younger than the man, will settle on just about the first suitable person she comes across. What is surprising about these findings is not that they are precisely what one would expect, but that they correspond so accurately to the ideal image. She is in her late teens, meets and falls in love with a man who is three or four years older, they get engaged, save up and plan their wedding and by the time she is twenty-one, they've married and settled down. What happens after that bears little relationship to any stereotyped ideal, but the foundations of what Germaine Greer calls 'The Middle Class Myth of Love and Marriage' are firmly laid down.

Greer refers to the wedding as the "chief ceremony of the middle class mythology" and interprets it in largely economic terms. She sees the big white wedding as symbolic of the couple's entry into the middle class and as an excuse for the respective families to display their prosperity. Money does indeed play a large part in the proceedings, but I would incline to the view that the white wedding ritual is performed for the sake of the bride – and her mother. For many girls their fantasies revolve not around the man of their dreams but around the dress, the flowers, the hymns, the guest and present lists, the bridesmaids and the speeches and the whole display that attends the ritual.

The 1972 British Medical Association's booklet 'Getting Married' truly reflects the real significance of the wedding, rather than marriage itself. The booklet devotes eighteen pages to the wedding, compared with a mere twelve on getting on together, nine on home-making and six each to starting a family, food, fitness, and, lastly, birth control. The booklet coyly tells of a girl who "everyone thought was not particularly interested in men. But a young man fell head over heels in love with her, and then we found she had had the details of the wedding planned since she was ten – down to the youngest bridesmaid's shoes!" Dead right she wasn't interested in men. She was interested in weddings. 'Getting Married' is, itself, an emphatic affirmation of those values. It is a call to arms to all girls to abandon any lingering notions of self-realisation so that they might apply themselves to the all important business of getting wed. The booklet comes out every year, has enormous sales and distribution and takes its place alongside *Woman's Own* on every magazine counter.

The wedding, as the one really significant and symbolic act which women take part in, is taken to heart by more people than the British Medical Association. The countdown to the big day, beginning at least six months before the appointed date, is a regular feature in every woman's magazine. It has even been known to creep into the school curriculum. One such school in the North of England, having taken as gospel the Newsome Report on Education which stated categorically that marriage was a vocation for girls, decided to put its ethics into practice. Every year, the school leavers take part in a mock wedding ceremony, complete with organist, wedding dress and ring. The girls weep and the boys look suitably embarrassed.[1]

The wedding is the culmination of all that the girl has been conditioned to believe about herself. She hands over her identity to her husband in exchange for a small portion of his, she takes his name and promises to love, honour and obey and she listens while the vicar pronounces them, not 'husband and wife', not 'man and woman' but 'man and wife'. The ritualistic incantation of these words, which define her inferior status not in the eyes of God but in the eyes of the world, must be accompanied by as much physical adornment as possible. This is the *real* purpose of the display – the long white cover-all dress, the face hidden by a veil and the bent head. In this disguise, she enters the church as a woman and emerges as a wife. The more beautiful she looks in this disguise, the more profuse are the tears. We weep for joy. Will she ever again know such happiness as she has known on this, her greatest day? Probably not. So she will treasure her memories, wrap the dress in tissue and pore over the photographs till the end of her life.

Marriage provides a woman with a name, status, occupation, territory and identity. With amazing sincerity, 'Getting Married' gives a step by step guide to wifely self-denial, steam rollering its way over the woman's emotions, potential and talents in an effort to persuade her that self-negation, when it is in the cause of husband bolstering, is self-enhancement. Under the heading "True Togetherness", it suggests enthusiastically:

> ‹Work at making your husband feel necessary in every aspect of your life together, and identify yourself as deeply as you can in all his interests. Even if you can't participate in his sport you can be there to cheer him on. Even if you perish the thought of his whippet or his stamp collection you can feed the creature cheerfully and put up with his bits of gummy paper about the place. Most important, pay your husband the compliment of really listening to what he says.›

Slavish adoration, mindless acceptance of male superiority and compromise of the female identity in the service of the husband's are the formulas for the sound marriage. Under the heading "He's Got to Come First", we find:

> ‹He's going to be first in your life now . . . The ideal aim is to turn as many of his interests as you can into your own interests and to keep on showing him in practical ways that you are interested in him.›

Is being a shadow enough? No, she has to be 'A Friend and Mother' as well:

> ‹Don't compare him unfavourably with other, apparently more successful men. Don't want to be right so much that you insist on putting him in the wrong, especially in public. And anyway, could it sometimes be your fault?›

Oh yes! Every time! Protect, bolster and massage the

male ego at all times but especially when it is at the expense of the woman's. The husband is at perfect liberty to contradict his wife in public because she has no separate identity. With the woman's ego to add to their own, many men can lie easy in their beds, feeling themselves twice the men they really are.

In case, with all this talk of female liberation, their women readers were getting ideas above their wifely station in life, the magazine *Woman*, reminded them that:

‘Every man would like to be 'top dog' and, although he knows few achieve such status in his own working environment, he can go on hoping. And while he hopes, he insists on having top slot in one area of his life – his home. At home, in fact, you may take most of the major decisions but letting him believe he's in full charge is a very subtle part of your role as an understanding mate. Your position is more difficult, naturally, if you earn more than he does at work. But there are practical solutions to the problem. However successful you are in the outside world, your aim should be to show by your attitude at home that he comes first and foremost in your life.’[2]

The article goes on to tell, in admiring terms, of a woman who earned considerably more than her husband, and describes the lengths to which she went to convince him that he was the breadwinner and that her income "was no more than an acceptable bonus to his". The perfect wife must not only be adept at disguise, compromise and manipulation, she must also practise the dishonesty code. A flash of the eyelashes, a purr of satisfaction and a liberal sprinkling of deceit:

57

‹It would help to display some deliberate imperfections from time to time if you think he is under the impression that you are pulling the greater weight in the marriage.›[3]

The woman who has swallowed the loving-wife line tries desperately to come up for air. How can she be the whole person she feels herself to be, when all she's good for is as a male ego prop? And when, after six months or a year of marriage, she finds that she can no longer live in opposition to her self, she must either capitulate or confront her 'problem'. Some women write desperate letters to the problem pages, but most survive silently in defeat. And the advice given to the problems succour those in defeat, a showcase for female subjection. Evelyn Home must have jumped for joy when she received the following letter:

‹Colin and I got married seven months ago and to be honest it seems like seven years. He wants me to stay on full time at work for at least another two years, but he doesn't stop to think that I get dead tired and could do with a bit of help. We live in a six roomed house and I do all the cooking, cleaning, washing and ironing while he sits watching me. He wonders why I fall asleep when we go out, but if I ask him to help he says "Just wait until this film ends" or "Hold on while I have a cigarette." I start work at 7.30 a.m. and am still on the go after 11 at night. He goes off to bed when he feels like it and expects me to do the same but how can I? He leaves his things all over the place and I sometimes think he's only doing it to get me mad.›[4]

Is she advised to bawl him out? Withdraw her services? Leave home? No. He's O.K. It's *her* who needs to change. First she's told how to rationalise the housework and then, unbelievably, "Kiss him often, praise him when he co-operates, curb your own desire to keep everything looking new and suggest that you change to a part time job." And "Cheer up". The message, as always, is that the man's freedom must remain perfectly intact while the woman finds new and ever more ingenious ways to deepen her oppression.

The magazine image of marriage presents society's version of the ideal wife. Whether or not women's lives correspond to the ideal, its impact on their view of themselves is considerable; it beckons to them all the time and tells them that if they're not satisfied they must try harder to aspire to the ideal. But the more time she spends building her husband up, the less there is of her for him to knock down. The woman's identity is eroded commensurately with the growth of the man's. The ideal selfless woman is a woman without a self.

The woman builds her life on the assumption that her husband's job or career must take first consideration, even in cases where she has a satisfying job of her own. Mrs. Neal, 'a career woman', interviewed by Rhona and Robert Rapoport, says:

> 'The wife must put her husband's career first. If you marry a husband who is a geographer or an archae-ologist, you've just got to adjust yourself to the fact of living abroad if necessary and giving up one's own job.'

As a civil servant, working in the same high capacity as her husband and earning a similar amount of money, Mrs. Neal is theoretically in a position where she could question the assumption that the husband's occupation must always take priority. When the economic necessity is removed, the psychological barrier remains. The act of putting the husband's occupation first is one of the determining features in the woman's attitude to him and to herself. A state of affairs in which the sex roles were reversed, where men willingly uprooted themselves, leaving their work, their friends and their social life in order to trail after the woman because she found a better job in another town and where he would live in social isolation, is inconceivable.

Much of a woman's identity is expressed in her choice of friends, her relationships, her interests and her private fantasies. Even the most determined woman can find her identity swamped by social pressure to adjust to the marital norm. She stands aside to watch her husband grow, while all the tangible evidence for her separate existence gradually recedes into the past or is swallowed up by domesticity. The process of losing touch with one's former self is experienced differently, but some features are common to many marriages.

‘I've lost track of my friends since I've been married. I've tended to take on more of his friends. In fact, to tell the truth, I hardly ever see mine.’[5]

‘I've kept in touch with two friends I had before marriage. Oh, yes, I do ring them occasionally.’

‘I'm more friendly with his friends than he is with mine. You have to be.’

Some women may succeed in keeping or making friends, independently of their husbands, but few are able to resist the heavy social pressure to abandon their outside interests so that they can better accommodate and encourage their husbands'.

‘I used to walk a lot but he doesn't care for it so I don't do that so much now.’

‘("Have you any special interests of your own?") No I haven't. ("Before you were married?") I used to love to go dancing.’

‘I used to read a lot but now I find I never seem to have enough time so I tend now, and it's probably become a habit, I tend now to sit and read newspapers. ("Husband's interests?") He's got a vast amount of interests but they're all in some way connected to his job. ("Do you take part in them?") Of course.’

‘He does loads of things. He's in a pipe band and he's just started fishing and he's got his aquarium. ("Do you take part in his interests?") I always go to the pipe parades. ("Any of your own?") Well, you could say I was a TV fanatic. ("Any before you were married?") I used to like to go dancing. I used to go very regular like but you give that up when you get married, don't you?’

This rejection of their own world, their friends and their activities is not only regarded as perfectly ordinary but *desirable*. It is the woman's public demonstration of her part of the marriage contract. In addition, her opinions, tastes and political affiliations all get diluted and eventually swallowed up in the marital machine. When she is trained to lack assertiveness and self-confidence, it's all too easy to agree with her husband's views, echo them in public and finally adopt them as her own. Often this unanimity – this 'we-ness' – goes under the guise of the composite married couple/one person syndrome; that is, they appear to be two halves of one person with the same tastes, the same opinions, the same interests and the same world view. Only it is *his* world view.

Marriage involves a strict but fairly unconscious regime of self-denial for women. It results in an opening up of horizons for men and a drastic reduction for women. The areas in which she is allowed to find satisfaction are rigidly controlled by her domestic supportive function and the years spent performing that role undermine her being to such an extent that she ceases to regard herself as a separate person.

‘Frank persuaded me to go to this conference on health foods. He was going to go himself but at the last moment he couldn't make it. He knew I might be interested in it so he persuaded me to go. Well, in the end I went. By myself. It was the first time I'd been anywhere proper without him. I couldn't get used to it for ages. It was funny though. He said I came back a different person.’

When other people regard her as part of her husband's luggage, that is how she regards herself, which makes it almost impossible for her to undertake separate activities or have any clear image of herself which is not overshadowed by her husband. And she is so practised at believing in someone else, that she cannot resurrect any belief in herself:

‘I would be absolutely petrified about getting a job. I would feel totally incapable of holding a job down. Honestly, I think I'm unemployable. I haven't got anything that's of cash value. I'm quite serious about that. On the other hand I see other people doing jobs – like the people in TV and I think "Christ I could run rings round them."’

The gap between the known potential – who you once were and once wanted to be – and what your housewife role has turned you into, is enormous and, in many cases, unbridgeable. The hordes of happy housewives that every man testifies to, when the role of women is being discussed, are simply those women who have successfully forgotten who they might have been. The act of forgetting is their only contribution to the world.

* * * * * * *

Status

"In order to get a clear rating for the patient's level of social achievement, they had to exclude all women, as no adequate system of assigning socio-economic position to women could be discovered."[1]

ACCORDING to popular usage, the housewife category covers all married women, not just those who work full time in the home. Statements like "Housewives will have to pay more for their butter this year" are commonplace; so also are newspaper articles which begin "Housewife Mrs. John Smith . . ." and only later in the article will it transpire that she does a full time job outside the home. Whatever their social class and outside occupation, all women become housewives on marriage, so that Mrs. Henry Ford and Mrs. Joe Bloggs, judging from the media image, have an awful lot in common. They are members of a sub-species of society who share the same non-status, preoccupations and needs. They can be referred to in the same breath because there is a dominant image of a composite figure called 'the housewife'. There is no male equivalent for the term 'housewife' because, unlike women, men cannot be conveniently lumped together as a special breed, labelled accordingly and dismissed.

Empty tributes to the equal status of women with their husbands might be more convincing if, occasionally, the imbalance was corrected so that we could read newspaper accounts of "Hairdresser's husband, Mr. Ann Brown . . ." or "Housewife's husband, Mr. Jane Smith . . ." or, even, "Husbands will have to pay more for their beer."

The term 'housewife' is not, then, the innocuous

65

descriptive word it appears to be. It does not describe a *person*, it defines a *situation*. The whole woman is defined only in terms of her relation to someone and something else. When the sociologist, Talcott Parsons states "The woman's fundamental status is that of her husband's wife, the mother of his children" he is not being academic. He is holding up a mirror to women's actual experience of themselves.

Following a TV programme on unemployment, Mrs. Maire Davies wrote a letter to the *Radio Times* vividly comparing the housewife's situation with that of the man on the dole:

‘It is a terrible thing to see a man break down mentally and emotionally. But the rate of mental breakdown among women is still much higher than it is among men, and some of the pressures women are subjected to are surely very similar to those affecting the unemployed: the isolation, the sense of being utterly useless to the community at large, especially when children are grown up; dissatisfactions at talents wasted; boredom; a sense of restriction and envy of others who are independent and able to travel about; above all, the total and sometimes humiliating financial dependence on somebody else – just like being on the dole.’[2]

Further on in her letter Maire Davies refers to unemployment as 'a social evil'; its effects on society are recognised and felt. It threatens stability and the social order. Government Departments announce figures, editorials are written, TV documentaries are made, men's dignity and self respect is lost and the country is going to the dogs. Maire Davies draws an exact parallel between the man on the dole and the housewife but whereas his situation is a public scandal, hers is a private problem. When society denies status to housewives, it also denies them any social significance. Where the man on the dole is the subject for serious public concern, the woman at home is merely insulted with propaganda telling her how happy and fulfilled she is.

The myth of equality of status in marriage is given its full weight, and is eagerly expounded, by every so-called expert on marriage and the family, from eminent psychiatrists to dewy-eyed sociologists, all of whose books begin with this triumphant, recurring theme:

> ‘In the modern marriage, both partners choose each other freely as persons. Both are of equal status and expect to have an equal share in taking decisions and in pursuing their sometimes mutual, sometimes separate and diverse tastes and interests. . . . With equality of status and mutuality of consideration they desire full ‘compatability’ in marriage.’[3]

No TV or radio programme or woman’s programme on marriage is now complete without the self congratulatory assumption that the patriarchal family system has long been overthrown in favour of the new modern marriage.

How modern is the modern marriage? And how equal is the woman within it? To judge from the torrent of words about marriage which regularly bombards us, one would think that marriage is some sort of *private* pact which takes place in a vacuum; as though the two people concerned really were free to work out whatever arrangement best suited them, without regard to social pressure and convention, legal requirements, tax laws, housing facilities and so on. The law does have a very deep interest in marriage, and the newly-married couple, intent on exploring their private mutuality, may be rudely awakened by the establishment's interest in them:

‘The status of marriage is one in which the whole of society has an interest, not just the parties in the marriage; quite apart from the religious and ethical considerations, both economic and social stability depend, to a large extent, on marriage and therefore any violation of it is the concern of the law.’[4]

Because the law is directly concerned with propping up "economic and social stability" and because such stability depends on the subjection of women, the law is a very real and identifiable arm of the State, denying women equality of status in marriage.

The pious statements of the pundits and sociologists on the equal status of women in marriage is revealed for the nonsense it is in a system where a woman cannot prosecute her husband for rape; where a woman pays the rates out of her own earnings and the receipt is sent to her husband; where her earnings for income tax purposes are added to her husband's so that he knows how much she earns but she has no right to know what he earns; where *her* income tax rebates are paid to her husband; where a woman must have her husband's permission to have a contraceptive device fitted into her womb or to be sterilised; where marriage denies a woman's right to have control of her body; where a working woman cannot claim tax relief for her dependent husband; where juries are made up of about 10 men to 2 women and where those women are probably widows or divorcees; where a woman is only legally entitled to half of the money she may have saved from the housekeeping; where a woman may not travel abroad without her husband if she is on a joint passport with him; where building societies only recognise a fraction of the woman's earnings; where she is refused hire purchase agreements without her husband as a guarantor and where the concept of 'head of household' (as the 1971 Census amply demonstrated) continues to determine the legal, social and economic condition in which all married women are kept prisoners.

Our laws, social codes and child rearing practices are all designed to perpetuate this condition; a condition which results in a state of mind familiar to many married women, in which they regard their husbands' duty to protect them as a prize they've won in a battle. But having allowed themselves to be co-opted into the condition women must, of necessity, salvage their identities and deny that they are prisoners of it. Thus, each woman is prevented from seeing that what may appear to be a private problem – shortage of money, lack of freedom, nowhere to go so that she cannot think of leaving her husband and overwork – is, in truth, a collective fact, shared in varying degrees by all married women.

Marriage takes the woman out of the mainstream of society and vests in the man the right to 'protect' his wife from society. He goes out to work to earn money for both of them and their children, he defends her against other men's sexual advances, he guards their territory and he stands between her and the outside world, both protecting her from it and mediating it to her. But why should half the population be in need of protection unless – and here the parallel is unmistakable – like slaves, they have to be protected in order to be kept powerless? Marriage for women, far from being an *escape* from the oppressive forces of sexual and economic discrimination that they are led to believe it is, is merely a more subtle rearrangement of them.

* * * * * * *

The
Housewife

Division of Labour

"If human endeavours are like a pyramid with man's highest achievements at the top, then keeping oneself alive is at the bottom. Men have always had servants (us) to take care of this bottom strata of life while they have confined their efforts to the rarefied upper regions. It is thus ironic when they ask of women – where are your great painters, statesmen etc? Mme Matisse ran a millinery shop so he could paint. Mrs. Martin Luther King kept his house and raised his babies."[1]

WHILE the man expounds on human dignity, a newspaper in one hand and a cigarette in the other, he lifts his feet momentarily while his wife sweeps underneath them. This "bottom strata of life" is time consuming, mindless and arduous work and women have always done it because their time has no value, their minds are 'inferior' and, anyway, who else would do it? Certainly not men, the sight of whom on their knees with a scrubbing brush or elbow deep in nappies elicits roars of laughter or an overflow of sympathy. By stepping down from the upper regions, a man loses the prestige and dignity which belong only to those who do not do their own dirty work.

It doesn't stop at housework. Men have to be protected from the hair and smell of women's armpits, from vaginal 'odour', menstruation and often childbirth. In medicine, where one would suppose doctors come into direct contact with things which would otherwise be beneath their dignity, it is the nurses who mop up vomit, lay out dead bodies and run the operating theatres leaving the men free to diagnose, prescribe, write notes and carry out the finer points of surgery and preserve their image in the bedside manner. Men resist contact with what they regard as the baser aspects of human life because they regard them as female concerns, by which they mean inferior. Indeed, many men directly measure their manliness by the distance they keep from these female concerns.

The division of labour between the sexes is not biologically ordered. In pre-industrial times – and in many non-industrial societies today – the division of labour between the sexes bore no relation to the significance we are forced to place on it. Evelyn Reed, drawing on historical and anthropological evidence, demonstrates this in her paper, *The Myth of Women's Inferiority*:

> ᶜThe men, it is said, were the hunters and the warriors while the women stayed in the camp or dwelling house, raised the children, cooked and did everything else. This description has given rise to the notion that the primitive household was simply a more primitive counterpart to the modern home. While the men were providing all the necessities of society, the women were merely pottering around the kitchens and nurseries.ᵈ[2]

This notion is cherished by the great majority of men and women in industrial society. Both sexes seek to justify the division of labour on the basis that it is historically proven to be biologically ordered. A moment's reflection would reveal that without industry, mechanisation, sophisticated medicine and so on, there can be no separation of the home and the outside world. The home and the outside world were one; real life was *domestic*. It was concerned with survival in a hostile environment and depended on the skill and effort of every member of the community, regardless of sex or age. To suggest, as so many modern commentators have done, that simple societies lived by hunting alone and that the women, children and old people depended entirely on men's hunting prowess, is to perpetuate the myth of male supremacy at the expense of the facts. Fortunately, there are some researchers who have studied pre-literate societies rather more objectively. What they have found is unpalatable for men which goes some way towards explaining why their findings are not popularly known. Firstly, there is hardly a single society which existed (or exists) by hunting alone. Hunting was most often a precarious and fruitless exercise and at best provided an addition to the staple vegetable diet, and skins and materials from which to make tools. These societies depended equally for their survival on the skills and ingenuity of the women who gathered food, hunted small game, developed techniques with their digging sticks to cultivate crops, domesticated animals, milked and fleeced them, used fire to cook and preserve food, made pots, wove cloths, cured skins, discovered and refined herbal remedies, built houses, reared the young and cared for the old. It is in this way that:

... the households they managed were not simply the collective kitchens and sewing rooms; they were also the first factories, scientific laboratories, schools and medical centers.[3]

In the light of this knowledge it is possible to see how cruelly the history of women has been distorted in the name of upholding male supremacy. We can now understand why it is that of all the activities necessary for survival, hunting has been singled out as the most prestigious and the most crucial when, in fact, it was often the most peripheral. We can now also see what a travesty has been made out of the division of labour between the sexes in non-industrial societies, equally sharing in the work of survival. It should be remembered that this is as true of so-called primitive societies as it is of many peasant societies today.

In industrial society, women's domestic function has been de-signified to the point where it ceases even to be regarded as work. This has happened for a number of complex reasons but the important point here is that it is a very recent phenomenon, for only 70 to 100 years ago, the woman's labour in the home was as crucial and as productive as her earlier counterpart's. To quote from Evelyn Sullerot's book 'Woman, Society & Change':

‘If one tries to evaluate the contribution of women to the output of a country, it would be much smaller today than in the Middle Ages, when women produced as much or even more than men. It would even be smaller than in the 19th century or early 20th century, since to the work performed by women in agriculture, industry and commerce and domestic service, one could also have added their numerous productive and manufacturing activities in the home, before the coming of the chemical, clothing and canning industries.’[4]

Modern industry has thus robbed women of their productive labour – it has refined it, mechanised it, profited from it and left her with the one function it cannot use for its own ends – child care. Women are denied full and equal participation in productive labour; their prime economic activity is no longer as earners but as consumers. Having taken away her productive and economic function, society must seek to find something to put in its place. It must compensate her.

A wide range of techniques for keeping women in

the home has evolved, varying in tone from the strictly moral to the straightforwardly psychological, and vying with each other for a place in the hierarchy of pressures which are exerted on women. Every social institution, from education, discriminatory employment and the media image, chases women into the home and then presents them with a choice of rationalisations for their oppression in it. A woman's freedom of choice, her triumphant emancipation from her past slavery, rests not in whether to be in the home but in which reasons she will accept for staying there.

Rousseau's oft-quoted dictum straddles both the psychological and the moral:

> 'The whole education of women ought to be relative to men. To please them, to be useful to them, to make themselves loved and honoured by them, to educate them when young, to care for them when grown, to counsel them and to console them – these are the duties of women at all times and what should be taught them from their infancy.'

We are in the arena of men's rights and women's duties. The woman's moral duty is to help the man pursue his manhood and her psychological satisfactions lie not in engaging in productive activities herself but in urging him to. But the satisfactions of knowing that it is only because she is prepared to watch and wait on the sidelines that he can play on the field is not always enough.

To keep her mute she needs to be assured that servicing men and children is a satisfying activity *in itself*. To bring it home to her that she has no choice, that her place on the sidelines provides her with fulfilment as well as

77

vicarious pleasure, society has come up with the ultimate device for keeping oppressed people in their place. It is the biological argument, seemingly inescapable in its logic and a certainty in its effects. It goes like this. You look at the function and consequent status of an oppressed group and attribute it to their genes. (It proved successful for centuries on black people until the emergence of Black Power.) But there has been no let-up in the use of the biological argument against women. Dr. Spock is one of the most recent in a long line of men stretching back through Rousseau, Freud, Byron, Nietzsche, Aristotle, St. Augustine and, most influentially, St. Paul, whose authority on the subject of women's inferiority would be astounding were we not able to see it in its true light. That is, that male supremacy only becomes a fact when women are inferior; the test of their inferiority is their relegation to domestic work. Dr. Spock speaks for many men when he says:

‹Biologically and temperamentally I believe women were made to be concerned first and foremost with child care, husband care and home care.›

By the same token he could attribute the function of black people in this society to their genes and say: "Black people are biologically and temperamentally made to service white people." The myth that women are at the mercy of their genes is as crucial to male superiority as it is to be the muteness of the female consciousness. The biological argument serves to strip women of the belief that their capacities can be directed into anything other than "child care, husband care and home care". What both male and female end up with as the basis for both their lives is that housework and child care are an *expression* of women's purpose and a *distraction* from man's.

78

This is the axis of the male-female polarity in industrial society. However much the man helps in the house he never invalidates this basic law. He may leave his own ground to share some of hers but he is not freeing her so that she can occupy the space he has left. This law insinuates itself at every level of women's lives, as the Rapoports found in their study of 'dual career' families, where both partners in the marriage pursued full time careers. In detailing the work and domestic worlds of these families, the authors found that the women took full responsibility for housework and child care, in addition to their own full time careers. The husbands' contribution, when evident, was almost always totally negative. Thus, one typical man's contribution to the running of the home and family amounted to:

&. . . he helps by not being too demanding, for example, he does not expect an elaborate dinner in the evening.**

When women bend over backwards to define that sort of attitude as *help* then we are truly in the realm of mystification. We are told that this couple spends Sundays, their one day off, "en famille", and only later does it transpire, in another context, that "Mrs. Harris cooks on Sundays, not only for that day but for several days in advance." The same pattern appears in another couple where the husband, Mr. Jarrett, freely admits that he is "the dominant partner in the marriage", by virtue of the fact that his wife, a full time television drama director, "has a separate domestic role which she must discharge as effectively as if she had no other occupation". We are told that "both at the beginning of the day and at the end she functions as her husband's wife in a near conventional manner". His dominance is exactly measured by witnessing his wife "discharging" her domestic duties. Despite the fact that all the women in the Rapoport study worked full time in demanding occupations, none of their husbands' participation in domestic work – and there was precious little anyway – was regarded as automatic. These men merely 'helped' their wives from time to time. These couples' lives, pioneering and unusual though the authors tell us they are, continue to adhere rigidly to the rules of male/female behaviour.

Ronald Fletcher, in his standard sociological work on marriage and the family, leaves us in no doubt as to what these rules are. After much repeated blathering about "equality of status", "mutuality of consideration", women's "equal right to pursue their interests and develop their talents", he does a complete about-face. Women's equality turns out to be as meaningful as the slaves' access to freedom. In fact one could, without loss to the sense of his work, substitute 'slaves' for 'women' in the following extract from his book:

> ❛. . . we need to give more attention to this position of the *majority* of women. They, too, have equality of status which should be made effective. They, too, are citizens who should have the opportunity of taking part in social activities – including wage earning work – in addition to their life and duties in the home. Women should therefore be educated for some appropriate pattern of life so that they are able to enjoy their opportunities to the full, but, at the same time, so that some activities are not undertaken at the sacrifice of others, so that rights and duties are balanced as sensibly as possible.❜

(To have to remind us that citizenship, while the automatic prerogative of 49% of the population, ought also to be available to the other 51% is a very real indication of the fact that it is not.)

Fletcher is merely Rousseau in a sociological disguise, standing from the pinnacle of male privilege dictating to women what their duties are, how they should be educated and how, if men allow them to, they can squeeze in a little bit of life for themselves, so long, of course, as it does not conflict with their servicing duties. We are left, as always, with a picture of men as human beings, untouched by domestic labour, and women as biological servicing machines, whose "rights and duties" must be "balanced as sensibly as possible". Sensibly? For whom? Certainly not for women. When we look at the balance of rights and duties we find imbalance, injustice and oppression. We find that women are educated, manipulated and mystified into spending their entire lives discharging their duties, in order that men can exercise their rights.

For those women who still doubt that a lifetime of housework and child care is their biological and emotional destiny, for those who wake up every morning with the conviction that cleaning floors, washing, wiping noses and cooking is not fulfilling, our culture has come up with the argument which finally gags and binds women and stigmatizes their demand for liberation as sour grapes. It goes like this:

‹The truly liberated woman is not the one who goes on marches but the one who is at the centre of her husband's and children's love.›

The invisible hand which grips their consciousness tightens its hold and becomes visible. The unanimous cry goes up 'It's all for love'. And the poor wretched woman who thought she was oppressed as a housewife hangs her head in shame. How could she betray her womanhood? To love and be loved, isn't that what being a woman is about? And even if she is still unhappy, isn't that the price women have to pay for their love? When the superficial arguments for keeping women in the home fail to keep her there, society bangs in the final nail. What we end up with are the three most powerful weapons used against women – male superiority, women's biological constitution which makes housework and child care the only thing they're fit for, and love. Women's oppression, their lack of real choice, is disguised by the illusory freedom they have to accept whichever of these justifications most suits them. In fact, they all fit neatly together and feed off each other so that, in the individual woman's mind, her role as a housewife and mother is an expression of her true nature, her husband is innately superior and the whole lot is sanctified by love. To admit unhappiness in her role is an admission of failure *as a woman*. To reject the role completely means that she is incapable of love.

* * * * * * *

The Housewife as a Worker

"Housework is the most unproductive, the most barbarous and the most arduous work a woman can do. It is exceptionally petty and does not include anything that would in any way promote the development of the woman."

Lenin

APART from her economic dependency, the housewife's most acute oppression is experienced in the work she performs. Despite the manipulative and profiteering efforts of the advertising industry and the giant publishing concerns to convince women that their work is meaningful and, most laughably, creative, nothing can disguise the fact that it is a treadmill, it is mindless, it is not recognised as work ("I don't work, I'm only a housewife") and performing it day in and day out, up to one hundred hours a week for five, ten, fifteen years without let-up in isolation, has incalculable consequences on the person who performs it. Everything about the work prevents her from developing who she is or might be. She is ruled by her function. Her work is maintenance. So she comes to see the home as the base from which *other* people's lives are lived – the lives of her husband and children. She maintains something whose only function, it seems, is to be maintained. She is in the position of a man who buys a car and devotes himself entirely to servicing it, without ever driving it.

There is no other occupation which is comparable. It has often been suggested by opponents of women's liberation that the great majority of men also work at mindless and repetitive jobs. Because there is some truth in the comparison, women are led to believe that they have less to complain about than men. This comparison between the outside worker and the housewife needs to

83

be explored, partly because it is used so effectively against women but mostly because it is wrong.

To take the outside worker first: millions of people set off every morning to sit or stand all day at a factory bench, behind a shop counter, conveyor belt or assembly line.* The conveyor belt keeps moving, the customers keep coming and the constant noise, the supervisor's watchful eye and the nature of the work itself are such that the worker is faced with a really soul destroying situation, a situation which, instead of demanding interest and involvement, demands the reverse. In order to prevent his soul being destroyed, he leaves it behind. Polly Toynbee in her book 'A Working Life', explored this. She worked at a variety of jobs over a long period – as an orderly in a hospital and as a hand in several different factories and she found, as all the workers could have told her, that such work is inhuman. It denies every facet of humanity – the need to feel involved, the need for personal achievement, the need to feel that one's day has been spent in socially useful and productive work. To survive in these conditions, the worker suspends his humanity; he switches off. But the nature of the work demands the minimum of concentration and the maximum of attention. This distinction is crucial because it

---

* Remembering the concentration of women workers in the unskilled branches of labour and that they comprise over a third of the industrial workforce and just under a half of service workers. But as the argument that the husband is more oppressed at work than his wife is at home centres on the fact that only men go out to work, I can only counter the argument on that basis. What is also conveniently forgotten is that there are at least as many men who work in semi-professional and professional occupations which are not at all boring and mindless. No-one would dare compare the professional man's situation with the housewife's.

prevents the worker from switching off effectively. He cannot keep himself intact. The net result, as Polly Toynbee found, is that doing a dull, boring job makes for a dull, boring person.

Now, all this applies equally to the housewife but the comparison falls down on several points. First is the fact that, unlike the outside worker, the housewife never ceases to be a housewife. She is not released from her imprisonment at six o'clock. She cannot punch her card and sigh with relief. She is not free to assume her real self at the end of the working day *because it has no end*. Most important, she cannot depend for sustenance on the knowledge that her working life and her private life are quite separate. Her working life is her private life.

The outside worker is not afraid to admit that his work is meaningless and unrewarding. He would laugh himself stupid if anyone told him that it offered complete happiness and fulfilment. So he looks eagerly for satisfactions elsewhere – in his family, in sport, drink or indeed in anything which is unconnected with his work. But the woman cannot laugh when she is told her job offers complete fulfilment.

There is no division between work and leisure for the housewife. Her 'leisure' is spent at her place of work which destroys any possibility of her ever forgetting it. Even supposing she were able to enjoy three or four hours of leisure in the evening, she is surrounded by evidence of her work role. While she is talking with her husband or watching television she is minutely aware of her responsibilities – the ashtrays which must be emptied, the cups and glasses which must be washed, the husband's and children's clothes which must be sorted for the morning and she must break off a conversation to put a note out for the milkman and all the time she must remember what she has to do the next day – the child to the dentist, clothes which need mending, sugar which has run out, ad nauseam. She goes to bed and the evening which her husband enjoyed, or merely relaxed in has, for her, receded behind the weight of things she has done and things which she still has to do. The joke that the woman lies there planning the following day's menus while the husband is making love to her is no joke to the woman. Doing housework and being a housewife are indivisible. The nature of the work determines the nature of the person who performs it. Because she never ceases to be a housewife – and this applies equally to those women who work outside the home as well – she cannot turn her back on her role without turning her back on herself.

Being a housewife involves more than just mechanically performing a certain number of tasks each day. Like the manual worker in the factory, it demands the maximum of attention and the minimum of involvement. In order to keep a house and a family running, the housewife must spend her entire waking hours tuned in to trivia. She must, as one housewife put it, teach her mind to free itself from thoughts so that it swims aimlessly, so that 'it can be called into action by an alarming sound'. But while her ears are cocked to the antics of her children and while she is constantly in a state of readiness for any emergency, her mind is also occupied by the demands of the home. It is the effort of keeping the mind free from interesting distractions which finally saps her capacity to direct her attention to anything other than spilt milk and dirty saucepans. She cannot give herself to anything consuming, not because the tasks are particularly strenuous but because the energy needed to register them is. If she relaxed her vigilance, would anyone else step in to ensure there were clean dry clothes to wear and food in the cupboards?

There are people whose minds are dominated by the demands of their work – doctors, teachers, social workers, writers and artists – but when their work overlaps into their private lives, it is because it is interesting, challenging and recognised as worthwhile. But the housewife's preoccupations are shaped by endless petty necessities which demand complete attention but neither skill nor interest. It results in a gradual debilitation of the intellect. As Suzanne Gail put it in her article on being a housewife, it:

> ... has to be practised for a distressingly large part of the day, often leaving me too empty for real concentration when the chance comes.[1]

Because her day has been spent being pulled, nagged and twisted by physical and emotional demands, it is very demoralising to find, when the children have gone to bed and the day's work is temporarily over, that the mind cannot suddenly be triggered into constructive action. If she reads, the words swim on the page after five minutes, a play on the television is a sharp reminder of a task left undone and because her mind has swum aimlessly all day, when it is called to find direction, even in conversation, it falters and fails.

This phenomenon is understood and experienced as fatigue.

> I usually go to bed at nine o'clock. And don't ask me how many sherries I drink!

> I'm tired most days. Sometimes I go to bed at 8 o'clock.

‘Tired? I wake up tired.’

‘I hate to admit it but there are some days when I'm too tired to get dressed.’

Betty Friedan in her book, 'The Feminine Mystique' explored the phenomenon of the housewife's chronic fatigue. She found that it wasn't sleep they lacked but stimulation. She quotes many doctors, psychiatrists and the Baruch study of chronic fatigue patients, all of whose findings support the view that fatigue, when it is not of the normal physical sort, is a response to boredom and to "monotony unpunctuated by any major triumph or disaster". Though her work is considerable and often far heavier than the man's (especially the white collar man), it is not normally sufficiently burdensome to explain the fatigue. Friedan quotes an article from *McCalls* magazine which rightly states that:

‘. . . it is the boredom plus, of course, the day to day frustrations which make the average housewife's job more emotionally fatiguing than her husband's.’

Though we should expect the woman who has an outside job as well as her home responsibilities to be more tired than the one who spends all day in the home, this is not the case. The fatigue that the dual worker feels is purely physical – it can be cured by adequate rest but the full time housewife's fatigue is nervous and emotional. It is, as the Baruch study showed,

‘. . . a warning of danger to the personality . . . [It is] not that too much was asked of them, but too little.’

* * * * * * *

Isolation

THE housewife's demoralisation is intensified and made complete by her isolation. The outside worker spends his day with other people. Friendships are formed and broken, ideas and gossip are shared and there is always talk and joint activity. With only the radio and, for the mother, the incessant demands of small children for company, she suffers isolation without the compensations of being alone. She has no break, no lunch hour when she can rest and talk with her workmates. She is literally imprisoned, especially during the long winter months, within four walls, and the only prospect of escape is a trip to the shops, which, with small children, heavy bags and pushchairs and the effort of clambering on and off buses with such a load, makes it more of a test of endurance than a pleasant outing.

‘After breakfast I wash the dishes and make the beds. Then I go straight out and do the shopping. It gets her (3 year old) out. That's my favourite idea. Get out of the place as quickly as possible but then if I do that I always have to come back.’

In talking to housewives and from my own experience, it is apparent that it is possible to adjust to having no money of one's own, that the humiliation of being regarded socially as part of the husband's furniture can be overcome, at some cost, but that it is impossible to come to terms with the isolation and loneliness. This is something housewives wake up to every morning. Many aspects of their oppression can be put aside and labelled 'abstract' but the isolation is immediate. It is the single most vital factor in their daily experience.

‘The day stretches ahead in dreary sameness, with no possibility of anything unexpected. I would rather

89

listen to anything or nothing than Housewives Choice. The thought of all those millions of women performing exactly the same gestures as me, enclosed in their circular activities, depresses me more than I can say. By the evening I am battered down to size.'[1]

'Sometimes I think I'll go mad with no-one to talk to. My husband says 'Well what can I do about it?' And he's right, there's nothing he can do . . . There's so much going on in my mind, it all goes round and round in my imagination while I'm doing the housework.'

Depriving prisoners of the company of their fellows – solitary confinement – is the best known method for sapping their will and turning them into docile vegetables. Enforced isolation has such serious consequences that many women never fully recover from the years spent at home.

'It (being a housewife) makes people give up. It makes people give up caring what they look like, caring how they act, caring about *anything*. I think I only live when I go out to dinner or get taken out. That's the only time I live. When something's demanded of you.'

What happens, to adopt the old truism, is that she turns into a 'cabbage'. She ceases to be able to think and talk constructively because nothing in her world requires her to. What is there to think and say except 'Don't do that' and 'What shall we have for dinner tonight?' And when the husband comes home from work and all she has to say is that the butcher was rude and butter has gone up and the little boy fell and banged his head, isn't that what being a cabbage is about? People cannot function if they are deprived of *experience*, but when each day is entirely predictable and when there is nothing concrete to react to, nothing to get excited about and no interaction with other people, whole areas of the mind will atrophy.

One direct consequence of being confined within four walls is that the woman becomes abnormally sensitive to those four walls. The prisoner in solitary confinement comes to know every mark in his cell and if he's there long enough, may form some deep attachment to its smallest detail. So it is with the housewife. Her response to her confinement is to become obsessive about it. Because she is deprived of outside stimulation she looks for it in her environment.

There are all sorts of obsessive avenues open to the housewife and all are tacitly and sometimes blatantly encouraged by social pressure. Cleanliness probably comes at the top of the list. The mark on the floor, the muddy footprints, the spot on the shirt can drive the woman to near hysteria:

‘I can now begin to understand why a woman in a small suburban house with no infants to look after, who does not enjoy reading because she has not had much of an education, and who is intelligent enough to find neighbourly chit-chat boring, should carry the pursuit of microscopic specks of dust to the point of fanaticism in an attempt to fill the hours and salvage her self respect.’[2]

The housewife's self-respect hinges on external approval which, in turn, is dependent on demonstrating to the outside world that housework is not a utilitarian activity but a *moral* activity. If it could be dismissed, as it surely should be, as a necessary but boring chore, to be effected in the absolute minimum amount of time, then none of this would apply. The pressure to pursue cleanliness, for its own sake, is deep and virtually impossible to eradicate, as even the most determined women have discovered. To the question, 'Do you do the absolute minimum of housework?' the following answer was illustrative:

> ‘I probably think I do but I doubt really whether I do. I do many things which I would not desire to do and don't totally believe are necessary but because I think other people think they are necessary. ("Can you explain that?") I suppose some woman who came in from down the road and she couldn't see through the windows and I don't care but probably after she'd gone I'd bloody clean them – out of sheer – I don't know what it is – it isn't guilt – it's something rather deep seated and rather unpleasant that makes you want approval in a situation which you yourself regard as not really worth bothering about.’

This woman's awareness of the problem – and such conscious awareness is unusual – does not solve it. Rather, it is intensified. It may appear ludicrous actually to clean the windows in these circumstances but as this woman has discovered, it is easier to yield to the external moral pressures than it is to fight them. If she insists on satisfying only her own requirements in a wholly utilitarian way, she risks being labelled self-indulgent and immoral. In these terms, housework assumes its own rationality. I was reminded of this when I undertook these interviews with housewives. Almost every one felt obliged to apologise for 'the state' their homes were in, even when they were immaculate. It is as though she feels that outsiders, especially women, have X-ray eyes and can see into their souls and that the unmade bed or the ring round the bath, though out of sight, will give the game away. She must convince you that, though she readily admits to disliking and even hating housework, she doesn't shirk her moral responsibility to satisfy other people's standards and not her own.

Housework presents a whole world of rules and pressures from which men are wholly exempt but which can drive normally sane women into absurd depths of guilt. It is a tight, inescapable world in which every housewife is imprisoned and indeed, every married woman, whether she works outside the home or not. (As Pat Mainardi wrote: ". . . if anyone visits and the place *is* a sty, they're not going to leave and say "He sure is a lousy housekeeper.")

In practice what happens in my own home, in the homes of my friends and acquaintances and in the homes of the women I interviewed, is that we all do just that bit more than is necessary. On top of that, we make a special effort when we expect visitors and we apologise for the state of the place because even though some of us might pride ourselves on not caring about it, we know we are supposed to. In this all-female world of housework, a clean floor means a clean soul.

The rules of housework are determined by what is socially acceptable, and what is socially acceptable is displayed in every magazine, some of which, like *Living* and *Family Circle*, with the largest circulations of all women's publications, are entirely devoted to urging women to greater and greater heights of house-pride. Moreover, she has the standards of her mother and her neighbours with whom she is expected to compete, and the pressure of television advertising – "How white is *your* wash?" She has to capitulate to her house-wifely role or be labelled a social deviant, and so the vast majority of housewives work away in their isolation, trying to achieve other people's standards of cleanliness, knowing that the more they give way to social pressure, the more praise they will get and knowing that an un-expected visit will throw them into a frenzy of self deprecation. She comes to understand that approval depends not on exercising her talents but on being an efficient housekeeper.

There are literally thousands of women who have become so obsessed in their isolation that they cease to be able to function in it. Compulsive cleanliness, as in the case of women who are never satisfied with their washing up and have to repeat the process three or four times, is a common complaint. There are women who make their families take their shoes off before coming in the house and though this will bring an endearing smile from her neighbours, no-one would seriously think that she was ill. In divorce cases, husbands can often prove their wives' obsession with cleanliness amounted to cruelty. Two extreme cases on record are interesting; one, where the woman insisted that the whole family ate standing up to avoid messing the new dining chairs and another, where the woman had driven the family to live in the garage because they made a mess in the house. The majority of women manage to cope with the pressures without inflicting their private suffering on other people. They keep their preoccupations with cleanliness inside the boundaries of what is socially acceptable, but as that is already excessive, their obsessions do not make news.

Hand in hand with cleanliness goes extreme housepride. Here again, the supposedly healthy, houseproud woman, for whom the house is a show case and for whom every cushion is permanently plumped and whose mind faithfully reflects colour schemes, curtain fabrics and carpet designs, walks perilously close to dementia. She takes greatest pride in her kitchen. It is hallowed ground with every utensil in its appointed place and where the act of cooking a meal becomes a violation of order.

> ❝We went to stay with my mother and I never realised how bad she was. We wanted to cook a meal for the whole family – do you know she couldn't eat it and then afterwards she spent three hours alone in the kitchen, just as though she was trying to exorcise us.❞

But the house-beautiful is never beautiful enough. The woman in it is the prime target of an advertising industry which manipulates people's aspirations and then feeds off their inability to achieve them. She is bombarded with images of the home-beautiful in every magazine, TV advert and film. And the sickness spreads. Increasingly, television plays and serials no longer concern themselves with human affairs. They are more and more like furniture catalogues displaying the ideal kitchen, exotic and sumptuous living rooms and expensive clothing, with the actors turned salesmen. They swivel the deep leather chairs and stroke the ten-seater settees, urgently reminding us that it is the sets which are the real stars. Is the housewife supposed not to notice the contrast between the projected image and her own surroundings? Is she supposed not to be dissatisfied with her home, however comfortable it is? And doesn't the image have its desired effect when she turns to her husband at the end of the programme and says:
"Don't you think we need a new carpet/curtains/three piece suite?"

"What for?"

"Well," (tentatively) "it's shabby."

"I don't know what you're on about. It looks perfectly allright to me."

"It's all threadbare."

"Where? I can't see."

"You don't have to look at it all day – or clean it."

And she's right. The house and its contents are not the boundaries of his world. He barely notices his surroundings. The point at which her dissatisfactions with her home become obsessive is hard to define. Like cleanliness, house improvement is a self-perpetuating thing. The more you do, the more you have to do. Putting new wallpaper up reveals the drabness of the furniture, new covers for the armchairs means a new carpet to match and so on.

But the ideal home, once acquired, only exacerbates her condition for she must then keep it up to scratch.

‹I keep saying if I had a nice house I'd be at it all the time. I really would.›

The 'ideal home' syndrome serves a very useful purpose in that it encourages housewives to attribute their unhappiness to the inadequacy of their homes. I found this in almost all the interviews I conducted, from the woman who lived in a terrace back-to-back who, with obvious justification, said:

‹I know it will be allright when we get the corporation house.›

to the woman already living in a modern council house who said:

‘The only ones I'm envious of are people that have got their own houses. We're trying like mad to save up and buy us own house. We'll get us own house in time because we both want it. That's our goal at the moment. A house of us own.’

to the woman living in a smart semi who said:

‘Everyone says this is a nice house and I shouldn't complain but I'd give anything for a bigger garden for the kids to play in.’

The media image, combined with our value system, succeeds in preventing women from recognising that it is their situation which is at fault and not their surroundings. And their situation is being made worse by the increasing emphasis which our society places on unattainable goals.

Like cleanliness and house improvement, small children can also become the object of the woman's preoccupations. As society extends tacit approval to the woman who spends all her time and energy on her children, it is hardly surprising if her preoccupations with them become an obsession. This is an enormous subject which is discussed more extensively elsewhere in this book, but I want to stress here that the housewife's responsibility for her children's welfare can be so exaggerated that it ends up serving the same purpose as obsessive housepride – an apparent solution to her isolation. But she is faced with an impossibly difficult situation. Modern technology, far from relieving the woman from the worst aspects of child care, actually intensifies them. The modern home is a nightmare trap for toddling children – wide, low windows, throbbing washing machines, every kind of electrical appliance, light upright

97

chairs which can be tipped over by a 9-month-old baby, low coffee tables which fall over when you breathe on them, vast arrays of poisonous cleaning substances and so on. Every year thousands of children die or are seriously injured in the home and those that do not suffer physical injury have much of their explorative instincts denied. What they hear all day is 'Don't touch that', 'Get down', 'You'll break it', and 'Mind the stairs'. In these conditions, there can be no question of enjoying the company of small, active children. Child caring, in the home, as so many women have discovered, is often an intolerable strain and the tension it generates, combined with the mother's isolation, can turn the once happy-go-lucky woman into a nervous and over-anxious wreck. She never takes her eyes off the children, keeps them constantly with her and if she has friends they gradually stop visiting her because conversation is impossible. It goes like this:

"I'm sorry, what were you saying? Diane, do be careful with that . . ."

"Well, he said . . ."

"Please don't do that Diane!"

"He said . . ."

"Will you leave it alone . . ."

"He said why didn't we . . ."

"Would you believe that child? I've warned her I don't know how many times."

When the housewife's response to her isolation is not focused on some aspect of her domestic role – that is, when it does not take a socially acceptable form – it becomes a 'problem'. But it must be remembered that it is the *same forces* which drive one woman to be excessively houseproud that will drive another to alcoholism, agoraphobia (a rapidly growing condition almost wholly confined to housebound women living on suburban housing estates), dependence on tranquillisers or pep pills, physical cruelty to her children or any of the other manifestations of stress. (In 1968, 58 million prescriptions for mood altering drugs were handed out and three quarters of those dependent on them are women.)[3] The members of her family, her doctor, and the whole of society attribute her 'problem' to her inability to cope with the normal demands on the housewife. She is a failure and a blot on their world. Ways are sought to minimise the effects on her family – more pills, a week's holiday with her mother, a little part time job? Or else the woman is so driven by guilt that she keeps her problem to herself. She disguises her agoraphobia by never going out, she drinks in secret, hides her pills and so on. But as long as she directs her anxiety into her domestic work, her problem will continue to go unrecognised.

The housewife in her isolation is not unlike the chronic invalid, confined to bed or wheelchair and totally dependent on others for relief and stimulation. Every day is exactly like the previous one with nothing to look forward to and nothing to look back on, with the certain knowledge that she is standing still while the rest of the world moves on. She lives a half life which is marked out by pseudo events. The invalid gets very excited about the doctor's visit, interprets every gesture and expression, dissects and repeats everything he said and then waits eagerly for the next visit. The doctor's visit represents one of the only real events in the invalid's life, a tantalising glimpse of the outside world. The rest of the invalid's time is spent in waiting, brooding, half-read books and newspapers. For anyone who has suffered enforced bed rest for any length of time the situation will be very familiar. There is the crushing boredom, the irritability, the disproportionate investment of emotion into trivial events, the frustration at being at the mercy of events outside one's own control and the total dependence on others to keep one informed of what is going on in the real world. And with this goes the need to invest one's own half life with interest and significance. The housewife suffers many of the disabilities of the invalid, enclosed in a self-enclosing world which holds meaning only for the person in it. Excursions from it are only interesting because they are excursions. A visit to town, a meeting with an acquaintance – like the doctor's visit – become important events in an otherwise unimportant life. She cannot speak of these experiences because, though they are significant to her, they are insignificant.

So, when the husband returns home and the wife tells him with excitement:
"I met Mrs. James in town!"
"Oh."
"Aren't you interested?"
"Where's the paper?"
In the end she gives up trying to talk about her experiences because she comes to realise that they do not rate as experiences. She begins to understand that real events are defined by her non-participation in them. Even within the confined world of the immediate family, her function is to listen to the other members talking about their experiences. As soon as the youngest child is at school, her last claim to be heard is gone. What the child has done at school becomes almost as important as the husband's work. All the family, except her, now have a place in the outside world.

As with the invalid, with whom the parallel holds good, the effects of prolonged deprivation may be permanent. Once freed of his disability, the invalid finds it painfully difficult to pick up the threads of a whole life and, paradoxically, yearns for the insulated security of his old life. The housewife is afflicted in the same way. It is easier to live a half life and pretend it is a full one than it actually is to live a full one.

* * * * * * *

Time

ONE finger that is regularly pointed at the housewife by people who do not understand her situation is that her time is her own. She has no boss standing over her telling her when and how to do her job but, more than that, she is envied by the nine to five worker on account of all the 'free time' she is supposed to have. What this free time and lack of supervision amounts to is that she is free to choose whether to wash on Mondays and shop on Tuesdays or iron on Wednesdays or clean on Fridays. As for free time – with small children *there is no free time*. There is not one minute of the day that the woman can call her own time.

‘Like thousands of women before me I learned what it was really like to be at home all day and be that adman's dream – The Housewife. I learned that the freedom to do what I wanted at my own pace was illusory and I was a hundred times more restricted by a young child than I'd ever been in the old 9–5 days.’[1]

‘Joe tells me I am freer than he is – I can do things in my own time without pressure from anybody. But that seems to me poor compensation for the sameness of the jobs that require perhaps less than one quarter of one's mental awareness while leaving the rest incapable of being occupied elsewhere.’[2]

‘I think the notion that you can arrange your own time is totally false. I find it very hard because I was used to long periods on my own but the business of picking up and putting down and being endlessly disturbed is a very difficult time rhythm to adjust yourself to.’

‘What gets me down is that there's not a minute of the

day when I can have any thoughts to myself. I can't even listen to a programme on the radio or *anything*. She'll (2 year old) interrupt my train of thought and one tends to give up in the end.'

'I used to read a lot but now I find I never seem to have enough time. I never seem to have a long enough period when I can sit down and actually get into something.'

'I used to do a lot of sewing. It sounds daft but I don't have any time.'

'I just don't know what free time is at the moment. It's a chaotic existence. You can never get your teeth into anything. You can't concentrate on doing anything, even if it's just washing up or making the beds.'

With only one child at home it may be possible for the woman, by careful management and with the co-operation of friends and neighbours, to give herself a certain amount of free time. But what happens to it? She has to use it to do all the jobs which she cannot accomplish with a small child. She visits the dentist, goes to the doctor or the Family Planning Clinic, she has a driving lesson or visits a sick relative. One friend of mine leaves her child with an obliging neighbour one afternoon a week, not in order to follow her interests but to do her big weekly shop, having found it impossible to cope with her very lively toddler in the supermarket. The housewife uses such 'free' time to do the things which other people regard as *intrusions* on their free time and for whom the constructive use of leisure does not mean routinely attending to their affairs.

The only other time which is free is during the

child's afternoon nap. But how can one hour, snatched from a day of mindless activity, suddenly be used effectively? It can't, as this following description illustrates:

> ‘Worst of all, that oasis in the afternoon when Carl is asleep and I can at last get down to my books, I waste destructively by going to bed. I have usually reached that point of tiredness where it takes some moments of fumbling to fix a plug in a socket, and there is an area of buzzing and shimmering between me and what I am trying to do, so I sleep. But my dreams are of the things I am trying to forget; static dreams, like a nauseating plateful of steaming sprouts.’[3]

Sleep is this woman's answer to her demoralisation. That ‘oasis in the afternoon’ is as problematic for those women who do not have such high expectations and who have no desire to get down to their books as it is for Suzanne Gail. Here it is, all that free time she is supposed to have. Just what is she to do with it? She can sit down and put her feet up, read last night's newspaper, call a friend or simply brood on her boredom. But all these things are either guilt inducing or depressing. So she makes herself a quick cup of tea and gets down to those domestic chores which can better be done without interruptions from children. Of course, it isn't free time at all. The child may sleep but she is still responsible for it. She can't go out. What that free time amounts to is a brief but temporary removal of external demands. Paradoxically enough, the child's cry at the end of its nap is a weird kind of release from her own emptiness. Everything is back to normal again. And the presence of the child with its demands on her time and attention, obliterate her doubts and frustrations.

With two children, even the illusion of free time

vanishes. And any freedom to arrange her schedule according to her own needs also vanishes. Having two children fairly close together is considered the ideal family, the idea being that you get it all over and done with in a few years (at least seven years before the youngest goes to school); that the children can be play-mates (and there's no guarantee of that), and that if you're restricted with one child, you may as well have two. What is omitted from all this is that the arrival of the second child not only doubles the work load – and there's more than plenty to do with one child – but it shatters any remaining possibility of the woman's pursuing any other activity than full time motherhood. It might have been possible to hand over one child to a friend for an after-noon but *two*? Even the hour she managed to squeeze for herself in the afternoon is gone when there are two small children to attend to, each with different routines, feeding habits and sleep needs.

When the second child is born, the housewife's isolation and loneliness is masked by ceaseless activity. When she doesn't even have time to sit down in peace to a meal, she also doesn't have time to reflect on her situation. She spends her whole day doing two things at once. The *Sunday Times* appears to believe that mothers have four hands. It suggested:

> ‘Some mothers find a good way to keep a restless, jealous two year old quiet while feeding a new baby, is to sit the toddler close to them and read aloud to him at the same time.’[4]

Children under the age of about 18 months cannot feed themselves and it takes about half an hour to feed an averagely lively baby and about 10 minutes to clear up after it, regardless of other small children, herself or other adults. By the time children are able to do most of the basic things for themselves – go to the lavatory, feed and dress themselves – a process that takes three years per child, the woman's habit of doing two things at once and 'letting her mind swim aimlessly' has become thoroughly ingrained. Many women, after six years of this, are physically unable to sit down and relax for any length of time, even after the children are settled in bed. The house-wife believes, though she probably hasn't worked it out, that the more she gets done in the evening, without interruptions from children, the less there will be to do the next day. This syndrome has been beautifully des-cribed by the women of the Peckham Rye Women's Liberation group:

> 'Like a fever dream it goes on and on, until des-perately you hope that it can all be achieved at one blow. You lay the breakfast the night before, you have even been known to light the kettle for tomorrow's tea, wishing that by breakfast time everything could be over with – by 8 a.m., the children washed, teeth cleaned, and ready for bed, tucked up – *the end*.'[5]

The housewife/mother can barely keep her head above water and the constant harassment makes the media image of the serene, immaculate mother with the ideal house and clean children, who lays an exotic dinner for the husband when he returns from work, recede further and further. The impossibility of achieving that state drives her to even more frenzied activity and while she *has* to do two things at once, she tries to do three. (Question to anyone who hasn't been in the position: try bottle feeding a baby, stop a 3 year old from emptying a packet of soap flakes on the floor and answer the door – or, change a soiled nappy, stop the milk from boiling over and prevent a toddler from making a bee-line for the electric plugs.)

* * * * * * *

‘Often the only time you can really be alone in the house is when you lock yourself in the lavatory.’[6]

In desperation, some women walk out of their homes and their children for an hour, a day, a weekend. All they are searching for is some peace, some time which they can truly call their own and somewhere where they don't have to be the punch bag for other people's emotions. Most of those who leave go back. Where else is there for them to go and what else is there for them to do? If they don't go back, they know they'll end up in the same situation, albeit with a different man and different children. But most women never leave. They stay and seek escape in the lavatory.

‘Isolated, the only adult in a private house, the housewife is yet crowded by the emotional and physical demands of her family, by the unseen pressures of society. But although isolated, the housewife is never alone; her domain is the kitchen, the most communal room, and even the possibility of sleeping alone is denied her.’[7]

There is a world of difference between isolation and solitude. Housewives with small children are perhaps the only section of society who are denied time and solitude. A situation common in many households is the following – the woman, suddenly feeling that she wants to get away from them all goes off into another room – (in many homes, this means the bedroom). An alarm bell instantly goes off in the children's and husband's heads and one or other follows her in and says "What's the matter?" She has to find an excuse and says "I've got a bit of a headache". Everyone else's need for occasional solitude and time to themselves is recognised and catered for. Adolescents can go off and play records in their rooms, husbands can go fishing or for a quiet drink, but the housewife remains imprisoned in her role. If she wanted to go out for a while by herself – even if only for a walk – she would have to make arrangements for her family's care in her absence and she would risk endless probing from them. "What do you want to be alone *for*?" It's not worth the trouble.

I asked the housewives I interviewed whether they would tell me when they were last alone. The question baffled many, first because they couldn't remember and second because the fact of not being able to remember, was, in itself, a revelation.

❛It's funny you should say that because our Teresa (she's 14 now) goes straight up to her bedroom when she comes home from school. Just recently it reminded me that I used to do the same. I did like that time when I came home from school and there was no one in the house and I had it all to myself. I was by myself – do you know what I mean? I don't think I ever have been since then. I suppose you miss it but you don't notice it.❜

She misses it but doesn't notice that she misses it except in moments of distress when everything gets on top of her and she knows that the only remedy, temporary though it is, is to get away and have some time to herself.

The need for solitude is a fundamental human

requirement but when the housewife demands it, she is judged disturbed or abnormal.

‘There was one time when I was getting close to breaking down. I really needed a break and I told S. He didn't understand. He said he'd give me a rest and take over for a day or two but when I said I wanted to get right away, out of the house and away from the children, he got very mad. I mean what would have been the use of me sitting here in the house listening to him struggling with the children? I couldn't get any peace out of that, could I?’

The husband got mad because his wife's demand was unintelligible. He interprets her need for solitude as a rejection of him and the children, as a denial of her role. This woman's husband also misunderstood her need for a break as a need for rest from housework. It wasn't the burden of the work that was bothering her. It was the burden of *being a housewife*.

The popular conception of the housewife is of a woman whose emotional needs are completely satisfied by responding to other people's. She must, as the magazines put it, 'share in all their triumphs and all their disasters', a tap to be turned on and off for their every whim and emotion. With the doors to her emotions open all the time, her responses become mechanistic. She trots out the appropriate words and tone of voice automatically, like the domestic robot she is. "Never mind", "there, there", "that's good", "soon be better", "oh dear, try again" and because she is always on tap for trivia, she finds herself responding in the same mechanistic way to events which are not trivial, characterised by the 'let's-sit-down-and-have-a-nice-cup-of-tea' school for anything from a road accident to spilt milk.

Without time for autonomy, she is a sponge for other people's emotions and a springboard for their activities. If she denies her family access to her she is, in their terms, denying them love. To give way to depression or anger, to abdicate responsibility for their welfare, however temporarily, jeopardises their faith in her. She suddenly becomes an unknown quantity. Who is this woman who turns round out of the blue and says "Go and make your own bloody tea!" The family confers together and decides that 'something has come over her'. How shall they treat her? Just wait for it to blow over? It's just a brainstorm, a temporary aberration, an irritating interruption in their lives. They will wait for her to 'come round' on the assumption that normality means that she will return to being a backdrop for them. And pretty soon she does come round. The alternative is leaving altogether.

Many women have learnt to compensate for their lack of time, autonomy and inner privacy by immersing themselves in their families more deeply than they are required to. They fill the vacuum that is left in their own emotions by actually adopting their families'. The vicariousness of their lives then becomes conscious and manifest. They embrace their husband's and children's achievements as their own, they fuss and worry over the minutiae of their daily lives and demand to be told in exact detail how their days have been spent. At first the child (and/or husband) recounts his day with pleasure, flattered by her interest and concern. But what begins as a pleasant daily ritual, over the years, turns into an interrogation. The housewife projects her hunger for experience onto her family and they, in turn, eager to keep themselves intact, either begin to avoid her questions or resort to lying.
"Who did you see in the pub?"

"No-one."

"Was it crowded?"

"I didn't notice."

"You must have done."

"Well, I don't know. I suppose it was."

"And you didn't see anyone you know?"

and so on.

Her emotional investment in them and their doings eats too deeply into them. To protect themselves they shut her out, brutally completing the hatchet job that her role has made of her life.

> ❝I know they don't need me any more. I think I realised it quite a long time ago, but I didn't like to admit it. It comes hard. Even J. [husband] doesn't really need me any more. It all came at once. I used to do all his paper work for him in the evenings – he was working very hard – but now he's got a secretary, or at least a share in one. And the youngest, he went on to the secondary school and he's grown quite away from me. Children let you know what they feel. He doesn't even like me to ask about his homework. You expect it and you're pleased because that's what you want – that's what you've worked for but it still comes hard.❞

The same woman who, at thirty, is praised for being a loving housewife/mother, at forty-five, is accused of being an interfering old woman.

* * * * * * *

Redundancy

REDUNDANCY is programmed into the housewife. The peak of her usefulness, when her children are small, coincides with the years when most other people are, consciously or unconsciously, finding out who they are and where their talents and interests lie. The housewife's are decided for her, as is her whole life. But that life is over as soon as the youngest child is independent. Her descent into redundancy accelerates as she reaches her late thirties and early forties. In theory she should be able to start afresh. But how can she make a second start when she missed out on the first one? She has accomplished her allotted life plan and everything on which she built that life is in ruins. She has, with more than thirty years of life ahead of her, outlived the only usefulness which society assigns to women – first as sex objects and then as mothers.

This is where the cruelty of the biological argument, which asserts that women devote themselves to 'child care, husband care and home care' is revealed for the pernicious nonsense it is. The life expectancy of women in industrial society is over seventy years and all those people who condemn women to housewifery and motherhood should be reminded that women can only be usefully occupied in that role for about 10 years (at the most) – *one seventh of their lives*. So Dr. Spock, and all our educationalists, politicians and makers of public opinion will have to dig around to find some other activity which could usefully occupy the remaining six sevenths of women's lives.

The half life they have led as housewives, becomes, in their forties, a non life. Many women solve their 'problem' by going out to work. But what opportunities are there for women without special skills? No employer would consider training someone in their forties so any kind of career or satisfying job with responsibility is out of the question. Like the young woman intent in making a life for herself without chasing marriage or motherhood, the redundant housewife finds her way blocked by society's pressures. She is supposed to be content with 'taking a back seat' now that her main function is over. What is forgotten is that she never occupied the front seat. To get out of the home and into the world – to make a vital new start to her life means ending up in the lowest paid menial work, which is often just a mere extension of the work she did in the house. Overwhelmingly, the cleaners of offices, hospitals, institutions and other people's houses are married women in their forties and fifties. Those few women who trained for a profession before they had children may be able to return to their old jobs – teaching, nursing and so on – but they are only employed at the rank at which they left. They find themselves out of touch and painfully apprehensive.

The injustices and humiliations of their domestic role are not magically removed when they go out to work. Society decrees that their primary role is still as housewives. And they still *are* housewives. They rush to do the shopping in their dinner hour and come home after a full day's work to the washing, cooking and cleaning. The young mother/housewife dual role is replaced by the worker/housewife role.

‘I suppose you could say I'm bitter about it. Before I got married I was going to be a swimming instructor. I was really good you know. I had a good career before me. But we started a family right away. He wanted it. He wanted me at home. You don't think then, do you? I go cleaning now. I've cleaned my own house and brought up four kids and now I clean other people's. I've still got two [children] at home and I do everything. *Everything*. He doesn't do a thing.*

Doing two jobs – one for low pay and one for no pay at all – only exacerbates the oppression of the housewife. The advantage of earning money and contact with the outside world must be offset against the dreariness of the work and the double burden of doing two jobs. Doctors and social workers who pride themselves on recognising 'the malaise of the underachieving housewife' recommend that she takes an outside job, however monotonous and however unrelated it is to her abilities. In truth what they are saying is, 'The solution to your problem is to double your work load so that you'll be so busy that you won't have time to think about it.' It would be like advising the factory worker who hated his job not to jack it in but to take a second job in the evenings.

However, the urge to get back to outside work is very strong.

Office or factory work seems more annihilating because even less of me would be involved, but if I were given the choice between that or housework, I would rather be out working in any conditions.[1]

There are millions of women out at work who, though they may have no choice in the matter, still prefer the monotony of the factory to the monotony of the home. Of those who are in the home, Hannah Gavron, in her book 'The Captive Wife', found that 68% of working class housewives and 75% of middle class housewives wished they were out working. Investigations into the reasons women have for working are usually based on the ideological premise that they ought to be at home and that they will only leave it out of economic necessity or for 'pin' money. One of Hannah Gavron's most important findings (and most neglected) was that this premise, though persuasively disseminated, has failed to convince those for whom it is intended. She found that only a tiny minority of out-at-work housewives work solely for the money (15% of the working class and 6% of the middle class). Yet Unions, politicians, newspapers and the majority of men continue to refuse to take working women *seriously*.

With over two thirds of full time housewives wishing they were at work, and with the great majority of those who do work outside the home doing so not purely for the money, we are left with a picture which shows very clearly that the full time housewife is not the happy, serene and fulfilled person society expects her to be. The most telling testament to her oppression is the fact that the only way she can demonstrate it to a hostile world is to go out and do a dull job.

To stay at home full time is to be deprived, in a very real sense, of almost everything which makes life meaningful. The housewife is denied first hand experience – all that is required of her is her continuous presence. The work she does saps her of self-esteem and pride and it requires "less than one quarter of her mental awareness". It can, as Betty Friedan suggested, be capably done by an eight-year-old child. It turns lively inquiring minds into cess pits of nappies, potato peelings and shopping lists. The work demands nothing of the person who does it except that it is done. To be done efficiently it requires ceaseless, mindless attention and it leaves a mind that bears the scars of years of non-use and a personality that is shaped by constant trivial and vicarious activity.

Suzanne Gail speaks of her life slipping away "uncharted precisely when I am most eager to find out what I am capable of. I sit crouched in a chair, feeling all that useless power suppressed in me". Before she was housebound she "always felt, at the end of a day's reading, writing or teaching that I had somehow added to life, enriched my experience, moved forward in a quite tangible sense". As a housewife she ceases to add to her experience. She ceases to move forward. The only difference between Suzanne Gail and the working class housewife – the pattern of their daily lives is almost identical anyway – is that she has articulated what they know and feel.

* * * * * * *

Economics

"The truth is that family life will never be decent, much less ennobling, until this central horror of the dependence of women on men is done away with."
George Bernard Shaw

THIS "central horror" has been disguised as love. Man works for money and woman works for love. The different values placed on male and female work reflect their value as *people*. Man is the provider, protector and prestige carrier. In his active role of breadwinner he is holder and transmitter of the fundamental value on which this society is based – economics. Woman, on the other hand, has merely to be. She is the mirror which reflects and enhances his status in the outside world. She translates his outside labours into the value of love and caring. Where he competes, she nurtures and comforts. She symbolises all the values which directly oppose those which he must represent. *These different worlds are separate and often in terrible conflict, because where the woman only occupies one world, the man has a place in both.*

Even if she works outside the home, she continues to symbolise the female values of love and caring. Indeed her outside work is an extension of those values. The ideology seeks to ensure that women go out to work not for personal satisfaction, excitement or change or even for company, but merely for extra money, a necessary and brutalising addition to their supportive role. Only in this context can it be understood how the pay and conditions of women's work continue to be so dreadful and why trade unions persist in neglecting their cause. They will, it is thought, happily tolerate working in conditions which no man would tolerate and they can be mercilessly exploited as outworkers because they work out of love.

So it is that the suggestion that housewives should be paid for their work offends many people. To pay housewives, paradoxically enough, cheapens their work. When it is reduced to an economic transaction with all that that implies – definition of work, hours, terms of contract and so on – it brings the hard outside world into the home. In addition, the stranglehold that her labour of love has on her would be released and she would occupy the same economic ground as her husband. Their separate and irreconcilable worlds would merge, depriving the man of his role as provider and severely curtailing his economic power over her. To introduce payment for the woman's work is to taint love with cash.

To work for love would be an honourable thing if society were based on love and if we could all live on air. But the employer cannot say to his workers on pay day "Thanks a lot. I haven't got any money to pay you but I love you."

‹In a society in which money determines value, women are a group who work outside the money economy. Their work is not worth money, is therefore valueless, is therefore not even real work. And women themselves, who do this valueless work, can hardly be expected to be worth as much as men, who work for money. In structural terms, the closest thing to the condition of women is the condition of others who are or were outside the commodity production, i.e. serfs and peasants.›[1]

The ethos which surrounds the woman's motivations, imprisoning her in its assumptions, disguises her oppression by elevating it. The prevailing ideology ensures that she will continue to work without reward by entrusting her with motives which transcend economic 'greed'. She is thus not at the bottom of society's pile but, strangely, at the top. She may be denied and deprived of the means of self-realisation, of a right to an independent life of her own, of even enough money to take herself out to the cinema once in a while, of enjoying any of the amenities offered to the rest of society (including even her own children whose pocket money is their own to do with as they like), of self respect ("He'd never refuse but I always have to ask for money, even if it's only for tights or something") but, with all this, goes the compensatory knowledge that she holds a special place. If the woman's work and the value attached to it were held in equal esteem as her husband's, there would be no need to place her on a pedestal. It is contempt that puts her there and keeps her there and many women, through long material deprivation, come to realise it, just as they realise that the pedestal they occupy isn't worth the illusions it is built on.

The love that women work for is not the pure selfless kind that men would like to think it is. It is borne of necessity. It's the kind of love which the small tenant farmer feels for his landlord – a sort of forelock touching acquiescence. Because love can only be given under two conditions – genuine equality and where the person who loves is not deprived herself.[2] But with marriage as a system of male patronage in which the man receives the woman's labour in exchange for providing her with a roof over her head, food and clothing, the parallel with colonial slavery is unmistakable.

Oh, but it isn't like that! Isn't it? When the love that so thinly disguises the economics dies, it is like that, which is why so many women will defend their situation very strongly. And because they are trained to find satisfaction in disillusion, they may even boast of their position. ("Oh, he'd never let me go out to work! He says he earns enough for both of us.")

A terrible silence hangs over "the central horror of the dependence of women on men". There is a widespread and deep seated belief that housewives are very privileged to be supported by men, and any suggestion that they aren't is instantly howled down. It brings about the same sort of injured sensibility as witnessing a tramp spit on someone who's just given him a pound instead of saying 'Thanks Guv'nor'. How dare they bite the hand that feeds them? And any pity that might have been extended to the tramp is wiped out. Women must be seen to be grateful. If there is any pity to be shed it is men who receive it for they are the ones who are burdened with working to support women and children; but to push the point a little, do we feel sorry for the slave owner because he has to feed and clothe the slaves who work for him or do we pity the slave for his loss of freedom and economic independence? The silence on the subject is the silence of guilt.

Betty Friedan in her book 'The Feminine Mystique' steered well away from the subject though she exposed most of the myths surrounding the happy middle class American housewife. She strengthened the taboo by failing to mention the unmentionable. Similarly, Hannah Gavron's book, though written from a sociological and descriptive point of view, also failed to take account of economic forces. Her book claimed to deal with the "conflicts of housebound mothers" and she studied their social relationships, housing, leisure, their attitude to work, their relationships with their parents,

122

their husbands and their children – everything, in fact, which affected their lives except the effects of being financially dependent. Her only questions on the subject centred on whether or not there was joint discussion of financial matters and whether or not the women knew how much their husbands earned. Which is rather like suggesting that the slave's oppression is eased if he knows how much his master owns.

The silence on the subject is also due, in part, to the assumption that women are not dependent on men, that in fact the money he earns belongs to them both. The concept of 'our money', with each partner having equal access to it, is a comfortable middle class myth. According to Hannah Gavron's study, it isn't even practised by the majority of the middle class anyway. She found that over half her sample of middle class housewives were given allowances with which they had to make do. Only 44% of these housewives were in the position of "drawing on money when they needed it". And of course if the woman does not know what her husband earns, there can be no question of her sharing it. A survey carried out by the Child Poverty Action Group found that "Husbands who earn more than £5,000 a year are as likely to fail to tell their wives how much they get as working class men."[3] Hannah Gavron found that over three quarters (77%) of the working class housewives in her sample had a "regular amount from their husbands' pay packet each week and tried to make do with it". Only 23% "just shared it out as needed". It is clear that equal sharing of the husband's income, with the wife's free and independent access to it, is the exception and not the rule.

But the exception proves nothing. What I want to suggest is that the shared money ideal is precisely that, an ideal. In the modern marriage, which the sociologists assume to be the norm, the equality of the partners is as much of a sop to women as the equality of their access to money. Whatever arrangements and tactics are used to tart up the situation, nothing can effectively disguise her dependency.

> **'** . . . I am getting more and more dissatisfied with being financially dependent, not because my husband has made any difficulties about money or considered my 'contribution' in caring for the children as unimportant, but because I *feel* dependent. **'**

For a long time I made the mistake of assuming, along with everyone else, that when people asserted that in their marriage there was no distinction between his money and 'our' money, that this was true for all couples who subscribed to the ideal. It was only when I thought back over my own experience of such a situation and when I questioned more deeply that the politics of financial dependence became apparent. Loyalty and self negation are powerful agents of economic oppression. If any sociologist or interested person had inquired into the financial arrangements in my marriage I would have lain my hand on my heart and sworn that we shared money equally. And, in theory, I would have been telling the truth. In fact, it would no more have occurred to me to spend money on anything but housekeeping as it would for him not to.

Behind the ideal, subscribed to only by a minority of the population anyway, lies the reality, a reality in which the husband can spend his money howsoever he wishes but a reality in which she must hesitate before obliquely suggesting that she really does need a new winter coat, a reality in which she makes do because to do otherwise is to encroach too far into the man's rights. The only money she spends guiltlessly is on food for the family and clothes for the children.*

The myth of 'our money' is further emphasised by the ideal of joint discussion. It sounds nice in theory but what it amounts to in practice is the means whereby the woman talks her husband round, gets his *permission* to buy a washing machine, vacuum cleaner and so on. Joint discussion is not evidence of increased mutuality in marriage but merely an acknowledgement that the wife may have some say in how best to spend money on the home. He apportions it and she spends it *on his behalf*. But do they honestly sit down together and discuss how he shall spend money that is not meant for the house? Do they weigh up the relative merits of £2 on a horse or a pub crawl? And if they do, doesn't the ideal of joint discussion lose some of its rosy hue?

Traditionally, the man is supposed to have a better grasp of (non-domestic) financial problems and he can therefore reprimand her for her 'extravagance'. Perhaps she bought herself a new pair of boots for the winter or a gadget that would ease her housework. But would she dare to question whether he really needed a new fishing rod or whether they could really afford for him to go to

---

* I was first struck by this in teaching when I saw children from relatively poor working class families who were lavishly dressed and where the husband never seemed to be short but where the mother had barely two changes of drab clothing. She feels no guilt in spending money on the children but, like skimping on the housework, it would be immoral to spend money she hasn't earned on herself.

Wembley? This double standard operates in the majority of homes and anyone who doubts it should be asked to imagine what husband, however wealthy, would fail to ask his wife how much those boots cost?

The woman's economic subordination is matched by her husband's anger and indignation. Righteously he asserts that he gives her everything she needs. He works his balls off all week so that she can have the things she wants and if he isn't entitled to some enjoyment, just what is he entitled to? And the woman, hurt and defeated by such logic, retreats behind a wall of self effacement. All her lines of attack are circumscribed by her dependent position. She, too, works all week, but it doesn't merit the label work because it isn't paid. And, without a moment's hesitation, he can sweep away the nonsense of shared money, merely by stating the truth. He earns it and he *gives* it to her. Faced with the facts, she can only nag or whimper. Such are the politics of economic dependence.

Housewives, old age pensioners, students, social security claimants and single mothers have a lot in common. They are all supposed to undergo some magical reduction in their economic needs at certain crucial points in their lives. People on Social Security form themselves into Unions to fight for better rights, and pensioners, despite the pious statements of politicians, are recognised as an economically deprived section of the community, but housewives are supposed to thrive on having no money of their own. Until very recently, the wife had no legal right to her own money if she hadn't earned it herself. Even if she had managed to save a little each week from her housekeeping, that money still rightfully belonged to her husband. This law has only recently been amended so that now the housewife is

entitled to *half* of what she's saved from the housekeeping. In the hard facts of people's lives, this is all very
much in evidence.

But the evidence is disguised by the apparatus of
women's oppression which asserts that women don't need
money for themselves. And the degree to which they
internalise their oppression is evident from their statements on the subject.

'I wouldn't dream of spending money on myself.'

'Quite honestly I can't think of anything I'd
want.'

'I can't complain really, he gives me what I ask
for as long as it's reasonable.'

'I wouldn't know what to do with money of my
own.'

'He wouldn't trust me and he's probably quite
right. I'd go mad if I had my own money. He gives me
just what I need for the housekeeping.'

'I don't spend money on myself – it all goes on
the kiddies.'

'You get a lot more sensible about money when
you're married. I don't go wasting it on myself.'

No other section of the community turns up its nose at money.
The husband allows his wife just enough to feed the
family, thereby keeping the lid firmly down on the devil
in her that will rise up at the first opportunity and go on a
wild spending spree in town. And such mystification eats

into women's consciousness so that they will nod and say "Oh, I don't handle big financial decisions. I leave all that to my husband," ignoring the fact that they looked after themselves very well before they were married, they didn't have to hand over the management of their earnings to anyone else and they probably budget far better than their husbands anyway. The 'I-don't-need-money-for-myself' syndrome is a profound response. It is a telling indication of the depth of the housewife's humiliation. She says she doesn't need money for herself because *she hasn't any money.*

The housewife's deprivation is a matter for speculation but judging from their responses, they impose a greater taboo on it than they do to questions of sex. The self denial which goes hand in hand with their subjection is subsumed within the general aura of house-wifely sacrifice.

❝He'd never refuse but I hate to keep asking.❞

To avoid humiliation, she stops asking and prides herself on her ability to make do.

❝I sew my tights up. It takes ages but they're so expensive. Anyway, I feel silly asking for money for tights all the time.❞

When I asked this woman if she would continue to repair her tights if she earned her own money, she said "You must be joking!"

The protection that the man's wage affords her is supposed to extend to relieve her of all but subsistence needs. But the material deprivations housewives suffer is not always immediately obvious. For instance, the majority of my questions about the food they ate were dismissed by the working class housewives I spoke to. Not only did they not sit down to eat meals, they did not eat meals. As with the rest of their lives, they tended to make do, that is, they cooked meals for their husbands and children and nibbled as they cooked and dished them up. Not one of these housewives ate breakfast. They simply took sips of tea as they dressed the kids and served the husband. Their diet consisted, on the whole, of biscuits and their family's leftovers. If one takes notice of the happy family-type advertisements, one can see that the woman is almost invariably shown standing up while the rest of the family are sitting eating around a table.

In very identifiable ways the housewife's economic dependence lays to waste her adulthood. In public he must handle the money. At the cinema or at a restaurant, even in cases where the woman is actually carrying the money, she first hands it over to him so that he can do the actual paying. Men must be *seen* to be in control of it.

Perhaps most oppressive of all is the fact that the housewife is, at all times, dependent on her protector's health and goodwill.

‘I know we live quite comfortably but then I also know that it could all disappear tomorrow. I've no illusions about it. I live on a borrowed dream.’

She can never forget that the man can withdraw his support whenever he chooses. Similarly she is dependent on his continuing good health which is why those advertisements for life insurance, with a cross on the man's heart, suggesting a coronary at an early age, are so effective. But widowhood is only the tip of the iceberg. It is when the marriage goes sour that the full force of her economic oppression becomes painfully apparent. All her instincts might tell her to leave but her common sense urges her to stay. If her children are small her freedom of choice is restricted to the frying pan or the fire. Her chance of earning more than £15 per week are remote and the possibility of finding satisfactory care for her children while she works is non-existent, to say nothing of finding accommodation for a woman on her own with children. The only other alternative is Social Security which will give her only bare subsistence money and only under extreme duress. They will watch her and question her and can withhold her money at a moment's notice and without explanation.

Unlike the woman, the man faces neither social nor economic hardship when he leaves. The following two quotations illustrate two sides of the same coin and indicate the impossibility of achieving economic and social independence for women in this society, either in or outside marriage:

‘I was so naive. It took every ounce of strength not to go back to F. I was so keen to be independent and have a decent social life again but it was *awful*. People just don't trust a married woman on her own. I never got asked anywhere and the only men I met were the sort who think, just because you're not a young girl, that all you want is a good screw. They tell you all that stuff about 'Oh, a mature woman like you' while they are treating you like an imbecile. I wasn't looking for another husband – I'm still not – in fact, I'll never marry again, but that doesn't mean you don't want honest friendships and relationships with people. But I stuck it out but there were lots of times when I thought I wouldn't be able to. Another thing which hurt – all the friends I had when I was married turned against me.

All but one woman and that nearly broke *her* marriage. All the rest stuck to F. even though they knew it was six of one and half a dozen of the other. When you're married you're wrapped in a cocoon. You don't really come up against this terrible contempt that society has for women, especially women on their own.❜

❛I am living on my own with two small children, ages 7 and 6 years. I am receiving an income of £9.25 which has to provide everything for the home. I am in debt with no chance of clearing it on the above income, and my nerves are suffering from this situation. I have approached welfare offices, one department tells you to go to work, the Children's Department say my children need me at home, so they don't help. I am at my wit's end where to go. . . . We are not in a position to help ourselves, we are just allowed to exist and that is all. I went to work for three months last year and I was no better off because I was paying too much out in income tax, bus fares, a taxi to bring my children home, clothes to go to work in because I have nothing decent to go out in – so I had to finish work and go back to the Ministry of Social Security, and as in doing this I have broken the years, I have to wait another two years before I get another twenty-five pence extra a week. It does not matter what I have tried to do, I am no further forward than I was four years ago when I left my husband and as I grow older it gets harder to bear.❜*[4]

* This letter is published in the Council for Children's Welfare's *The Plight of One Parent Families.* It details the struggle which these families face in housing, child care and desperate poverty. Despite the neutral title of the Report, out of the hundred cases it covered, only four were men bringing up children on their own, only two of whom had been deserted.

In theory, the husband is obliged to pay maintenance to his wife when she has custody of the children. But the law makes it ludicrously easy for him to evade payment and in a very real sense condones his right not to. If he goes to ground, only token attempts are made to find him. The courts are lenient in other ways. Four weeks can lapse in his payments before any action is taken and there are many cases where men are hundreds of pounds in arrears about which nothing is done.

As long as society refuses to pay women a decent wage, sufficient to support themselves as well as their children, as long as it continues to assert that women should be dependent on men, as long as Social Security departments, employers, Housing Committees and maintenance laws deny women's right to decent food, warmth, clothing and good housing, married women with children will be forced to give way to their common sense.[5] They will be compelled to stay with their husbands for the sake of their children, that is, for their economic security. The Missing Persons Department of the Salvation Army has about four times as many errant husbands on their books as wives. We can only guess at the submerged numbers of women who are desperately unhappy in their marriages but who stay because economics has replaced love.

* * * * * * *

Motherhood

The Rise of Motherhood

> *"It has probably been the exception throughout human*
> *history rather than the rule for the biological mother*
> *to be the child's sole caretaker."*
> Jerome Kagan & Philip Whitten

WE need not be quite as guarded as Jerome Kagan and Philip Whitten. Not only is this practice of child rearing the exception but it is, today, practised by only a minority of the world's population and it is also less than one hundred years old. But our attitudes to child rearing, with the mother caring for the children in isolation from the community with nothing but an occasional helping hand and the odd dispensation of authority from the father if and when he's around, are fixed in the tradition that this method is the only conceivable one. This tradition embodies the comforting knowledge that our method of child rearing is universal, there are no other methods and there never have been. When such knowledge is challenged and shown to be quite false, strange things happen which further illuminate how firmly these values are internalised.

First, the evidence is rejected out of hand. Anthropological findings showing the multiplicity of child rearing practices, ranging from societies where every member of the group takes responsibility for children regardless of parenthood or blood ties, to societies where men watch over the children while the women work, are dismissed on the basis that such people are 'primitive' and that we therefore have nothing to learn from them. More often, the evidence is questioned. This goes along the following lines: 'It's all very well to talk about these other societies but if you look closer at them, you'll find the same basic pattern as ours everywhere, with the mother caring for the children and the father working to support them. It stands to reason.'

The grip that our values has exerted on us is tenacious to the point of blind resistance. If that resistance is dented a little, it results in confusion and insecurity, which suggests that our surface complacency belies a deep uncertainty. Why else attack the Israeli kibbutz system for producing 'unimaginative robots', or the Chinese communes for 'indoctrinating' their children. If we were so sure that our own children were not indoctrinated into the competitive values of our own society and if we were so certain that our children were full of unbounded imagination because they were spared a kibbutz upbringing, then our attacks on the child rearing practices of other societies would not be so vitriolic. The very last resort liberal people will unwillingly go to is to say, "Well, I don't see that there's anything we can learn from these other societies; bringing up children like that may work for them but it wouldn't work for us." Or, to put it another way, it doesn't matter what other methods there are for bringing up children; our way is the best.

Ellen Adams wrote:

❛The job of a value system of a society is to make things that are useful to it seem inevitable.**❜**[1]

But the value system, particularly in our very complex society, cannot be left to chance. Social scientists and policy makers continue to pop up to keep its wheels properly oiled, laying down general guide lines which persuade us, implicitly, that the social order *is* given in the nature of things and to ensure that we do not stray too far from it. The social order is heavily dependent on the willingness of women to be the sole caretakers of their children while their husbands go out to work. It is equally dependent on women's readiness to take full responsibility for their children when they themselves go out to work. By stressing the mother's sole responsibility, the system avoids providing comprehensive day care facilities, after school play centres, holiday centres and flexible working hours for men and women so that they can take time off when their children are ill, and increased child allowances. The mother's responsibility for children also 'justifies' all women being exploited as a reserve pool of cheap labour, as well as rationalising discrimination in education and employment and, in so doing, saves the State and the employing class a great deal of money.

The imbalance inherent in this aspect of our social order requires strenuous efforts to keep it afloat. Because it hinges on the woman as full time mother and father as full time worker (regardless of the actual *reality*, e.g. widespread male unemployment, working women), the subject of child rearing assumes a significance unparalleled in human history. No other area of the human sciences has had so much attention and no other human relationship has been so exposed to the probing interference of self-styled experts as the relationship between mother and child. The proliferation of manuals on child care, whose sales exceed those of any other type of book, is just one instance of this. The efforts of this large body of psychiatrists and paediatricians to shift all the burden of child care onto the biological mothers and to persuade them that they, and they alone, should be responsible for rearing the next generation, must be counted as one of the great success stories of the twentieth century.

But the experts who write so persuasively have overplayed their hand. If the responsibility for child care was as natural to the biological mother as they would have us believe, then we must ask why we have to be constantly reminded of it. Do we have to be told to defecate, make love or eat? What is certain is that the more we are nagged about the natural inevitability of our child rearing methods, the less inclined we will be to point out its deficiencies, its imbalance and its want of factual basis either in biology, history or anthropology. Nowhere in the popular or scientific literature will there be even a whisper of a suspicion that all is not quite as it should be in the domestic cave, and that the image of the mother happily tending to the infants while father is out working in the world to provide for them, is not the inflexible law of human behaviour that they would like us to think it is.

This chapter is concerned with demonstrating that not only is this method of child rearing not the best, but the very worst imaginable, that far from being a human absolute, it evolved as a response to the industrial revolution, when society moved from rural to urban living and when men became slaves to the mines and the factories and women became slaves to men and children, and that as that process has intensified – notably in the post 2nd World War period – so our child rearing methods have been increasingly and exclusively geared to the needs of a capitalist society. Our method is not universal, it is not divinely ordained, it has nothing to recommend it and, most important of all, it is high time the lid was lifted off it and the myths exposed for the nonsense they are.

It will probably come as a surprise to many people to know that the exclusive emphasis on the maternal aspects of child care is a very recent phenomenon. We only have to look back to the last war and the decades preceding it to see a very different system of values operating. During the war women's labour suddenly became vital and vast numbers were drafted in to work at occupations which, both then and now, were deemed male preserves. They worked in the munitions factories, they drove tractors and tankers and they worked in all the essential services. And their children? The authorities instantly found the necessary resources to build and staff hundreds of day nurseries where babies and small children were cared for while their mothers worked. And what of the older children? Many thousands were evacuated out of the cities into the country and thousands of families welcomed these city children into their homes. And have today's thirty-to-forty-year-olds suffered all their lives because they were deprived of their mothers' exclusive care and attention?

It is all too easy to dismiss or, more likely, forget these things because they happened under extraordinary circumstances and any lessons that were learnt from them – for instance, women's ability to do 'men's' work – can be shown to be inappropriate to normal circumstances. But normal circumstances, especially those involving child care, are subject to changes all the time. What was normal in the decades before the war would be distinctly abnormal now. A social history of parenthood in the twentieth century would reveal an enormous range of practices ranging from, on the one hand, the propertied classes who gave over the care of their children to wet nurses, nannies and governesses until they were old enough to be sent to boarding school, and, on the other, the working classes where poverty and undernourishment drove all the able-bodied out to work for long gruelling hours and where the care of the youngest children devolved onto grandparents, unmarried aunts and so on, while the older children avoided school and went to work. These different practices continued, in varying forms, right up to the war. Only in rare cases did the biological mother have sole care of her children.

The dramatic changes of the post war years had devastating effects on women. In the first place they found, with the men returned from war, that their labour in industry was no longer vital. Though they still continued to go out to work, their numbers decreased and the occupations they engaged in shrank to 'women's work'. The nurseries closed as rapidly as they had opened and women once again were told that they belonged in the home. But the home, as it was known and experienced in the pre-war years, began to look very different. It, too, shrank. The enormous expansion of industry, the necessity for a mobile labour force ready to move wherever their skills were needed and wherever there were jobs, the growth of the welfare state and the massive rebuilding programmes which cleared slums and rebuilt bombed streets in vast ribbon developments of small semis and replaced large Edwardian and Victorian houses with tower blocks, all combined to break up the extended family and close-knit street communities into the millions of isolated units we know today. Just as the working class mother could no longer rely on assistance from nearby relatives and neighbours, so the upper class woman found her previously inexhaustible supply of servants had dried up. J. Gathorne Hardy in his book, 'The Rise and Fall of the British Nanny' notes that:

‘In 1939, with the number of domestic servants still at about one and a quarter million, the number of Nannies, at the least, was some hundred and forty thousand; for reasons already given the figure was probably somewhere between two hundred and fifty thousand and three hundred and fifty thousand. The

War finished them off . . . even by 1951, the number of domestic servants had barely risen to half of what it had been before while the total population continued to soar.9

Elsewhere in the book he states that nannies were not expected to cope with children unaided. There were often two or three servants per child, in a domestic hierarchy ranging from governess, through nanny, down to nursery maid and cleaner.

Domestic servants are only available under two conditions – when there are very rigid class divisions, when society can roughly be divided into those who serve and those who are served and when there is widespread unemployment and poverty. The prosperity of the post-war boom years blurred these class divisions and virtually eradicated unemployment. For the first time in human history, women of all social classes were left alone in their homes to bring up their children without either the support of the family and street community or the assistance of paid servants.

But the supposed natural inclination of women to care selflessly for their children couldn't be left to take its own course. Society needed reference points by which to gauge acceptable behaviour in a time of rapid social change. It needed a theory which could translate the uncertainty caused by these tremendous changes in domestic conditions, into a stronghold of security. With no-one available to care for small children while their mothers were in the factories or taking tea in their drawing rooms, as if by magic, it became a terrible sin even to contemplate sharing or handing over the care of their children to anyone but the individual mother. With unions and industry zealously protecting men's

141

jobs, the notion that women's right to work was as automatic as men's died a sudden death. Motherhood stepped down from the idealised paintings in art galleries and invaded people's lives. And a whole generation of male child-psychologists found instant fame and publicity by creating the ideology to rationalise this state of affairs. Their dictates have succeeded in forming the pivots of women's lives, with the result that the hand of motherhood lies heavier on women now than ever before.

The man who gave substance to the ideology was Dr. John Bowlby who, in 1947, first stressed the importance of the mother's continuous presence for the child's well being. The fact that his work in the area of mother/child dependence coincided precisely with the post-war period should not be underestimated. In his important book, '44 Juvenile Thieves', he gave dire warning of the consequences of mother-child separation:

> ❛It appears that there is a very strong case indeed for believing that prolonged separation of a child from his mother (or mother surrogate) during the first five years of life stands foremost among the causes of delinquent character development and persistent misbehaviour.❜

He continued the work begun in this book and in 1952 published his monograph, 'Maternal Care and Mental Health', for the World Health Organisation, in which he expanded his thesis at great length in an odd mixture of sentimentality, dubious logic and straightforward prejudice. The wealth of articulate criticism his work received from fellow psychiatrists was drowned by the book's triumphant reception. His work was exactly what the world was waiting for. He provided a 'scientific' basis for what was, by then, the status quo; a ready packaged parcel of goodies which could be unwrapped and imposed on a lay world which was buffeted by social upheaval and by the death rattles of old traditions. The world listened when he said what had never been said before:

‘What is believed to be essential for mental health is that the infant and young child should experience a warm, intimate and continuous relationship with his mother (or permanent mother substitute) in which both find satisfaction and enjoyment.’

In the same work he defied women ever to leave their children in another's care:

‘Partial deprivation brings in its train acute anxiety, excessive need for love, powerful feelings of revenge and, arising from these last, guilt and depression. . . . Complete deprivation . . . has even more far-reaching effects on character development and may entirely cripple the capacity to make relationships.’

Many writers have attested to the devastating impact of Bowlby's work. In their book 'Working Mothers and Their Children', Professor Yudkin and Anthea Holme, with thinly disguised sarcasm, state:

‘Bowlby's hypotheses continue even now to provide both official and unofficial bodies with supposedly irrefutable evidence in favour of such money saving projects as closing day nurseries.’

And still, twenty years after the publication of Bowlby's work, Barry Hill could note that Bowlby's views have become "folk lore."[2] The anthropologist, P. G. Riviere, suggests that the significance accorded to Bowlby's work has become an inescapable fact of our culture and, as far as its impact on shaping our thought and behaviour is concerned, must take its place alongside the motor car and the television.

> '. . . the importance of maternal care for the welfare of the child derived from him [Bowlby]; he gave birth, so to speak, to one of our collective representations.'

It is a "collective representation" because not only does everyone know about it (though the majority may never have heard of Bowlby), but they act on it. The debate that goes on in the learned journals as to the merits or otherwise of Bowlby's work – and his many successors – is of no consequence; it cannot make inroads into the public consciousness, because that is rooted in his ideology of motherhood which is now part of our social heritage, passed on through the generations. The difficulty of attacking that ideology, as so many of Bowlby's opponents have discovered, is that the onus is on them to *prove* him wrong, when he himself has never been proved right. No amount of reasoned criticism, pointing out the deficiencies of his work, its simplifications and its over-statements can reduce its significance so long as his views *sound* right, which they will continue to do as long as the social situation exactly mirrors his dictates.

By idealising the woman's relationship to her child, he exempted men from guilt over their separation from young children. They had had little enough to do with children before, having left it to the women in the family and the neighbourhood, or to paid female servants. It is for these reasons that the lay and professional world were so eager to take his views to heart, write manuals on them and disseminate them through

144

every branch of the media, with the result that we are now living in a climate of opinion which attributes delinquency to working mothers, which condemns women, whatever their personal inclinations, to stay home and look after their children until they are at least of school age and then to take only part-time work, rather than 'abandon' them to nurseries, their fathers' or communal care, and which labels any woman who does not conform as a cold and selfish social deviant.

This mythology has reached such extraordinary heights that all child care departments, divorce court judges and schools assert that 'a bad mother is better than no mother'. But how bad is bad? In 1972 a case of a battered child, who had first been removed from his mother's and step father's care, owing to their cruelty, was returned to them only to be beaten to death.[3] As a teacher in an educational priority area, I frequently come into direct contact with severe cases of child neglect and although such cases are known to the authorities, nothing is done about them. Only the NSPCC does its best by providing a week's annual holiday for the children. As long as the mother is present in the home, regardless of whether she wants to or is physically and financially *able* to care for them, the children will not be taken from her and placed in foster homes. Only when the mother finally deserts the children, probably after years of impossible struggle, will the authorities take action, often denying the father the right to keep his children together. When women literally abandon their babies and children on doorsteps – and it does still happen! – out of desperation born of knowing that they cannot care for them adequately, what do the authorities do? Find the mother and give the child back with a peace offering of a visit from a social worker for ten minutes once a week or fortnight.

The same ideology operates in divorce cases, where the custody of children is almost always granted to the mother. The following case, reported in *The Guardian*, illustrates the situation very clearly:

> ‛A father who had cared for his three children single handed since he and his wife parted 10 months ago was ordered yesterday to hand over the youngest child, aged 4, to his wife.’[4]

Despite the fact that the father had "looked after them well" and that "he had great affection for his young son", the judges decided that "mothers were naturally warmer in their treatment of children than fathers naturally were" and "though he (the child) *seems* happy enough it is nothing like as wholesome as being in the same home all day with his mother." (my emphasis).

Another such case underlines the principle that mother is always best:

> ‛Two Appeal Court Judges held yesterday that it was better for a boy aged two to be returned by his father to his mother, who had left home to live with another man. The boy, Karl Mounter, had been cared for by the father for 11 months with the help of a babysitter and *was said to be* very happy. . . . Lord Justice said he could not regard the boy's life as satisfactory, *however happy he was at present*. . . . A little child ought to have the warmth and day to day attention which a mother gives. . . . From the point of view of common sense and humanity, the place for a small child was normally with its mother, despite the most unsatisfactory situation in which Mrs. Mounter was at present.’[5] (my emphasis).

The Courts, in the grip of Bowlby's folk lore,

won't allow that either of these children could be happy with their fathers. The first child is separated not only from his father but from his siblings and both children are taken from homes they have known and been happy in for nearly a year – in Karl's case that is half his life and he is then placed in a "most unsatisfactory situation". And were either of these decisions taken, as the judges would have us believe, in the best interests of the child, or were they, as it so transparently appears, taken in the interests of upholding the values of motherhood? "Common sense and humanity", as the judges fondly proclaim, have nothing to do with it. Both these children were sacrificed to an ideology which maintains that the mere *presence* of the mother guarantees the child's happiness and well being, while the love of a father does not.

* * * * * * *

Maternal Deprivation

ONE finds, in speaking to housewives' organisations, student meetings, charitable organisations, political groups and so on that though almost everyone is willing to concede that women do 'have a raw deal', few believe that anything can or should be done about it. Such resistance to change almost always hinges on the belief that women can never achieve effective 'equality' because their children need them at home. Indeed, there is a tremendous reluctance to relinquish the values of motherhood, symbolising as they do, an island of love and caring in a sea of materialism. So any suggestion that children do not need their mothers' undivided attention is always interpreted as a frightening threat. It accounts for some very vitriolic attacks on the movement for women's liberation, suggesting that such women don't love their children and want to abandon them to 24 hour nurseries so that they can pursue professional careers. Nothing could be further from the truth, but the image persists. So the spectre of 'deprived' children always looms large among those who oppose the liberation of women. Not surprisingly, the misleading articles in the press do nothing to counter the popular image of a band of crazed women who neglect their children. It is for these reasons that I have gone into the subject of maternal deprivation at some length. But it is a difficult nut to crack. To disentangle the myth from reality, when those myths are part of our heritage of "common sense and humanity" is to assume the mantle of madness and inhumanity.

We owe entirely to Bowlby what has now become common knowledge, that is, that children brought up in orphanages *may* be deprived and may have difficulty in forming relationships. (What has bothered many researchers is that not all such children are badly affected, and much energy has been sidetracked into studying why some children are affected and others not.) But since Bowlby's work was published and publicised, children's homes, often working against staff and money shortages, have made tremendous efforts to humanise their institutions and the old style starchy matron dispensing authority and caring only for the children's physical needs in a near Dickensian environment, have transformed themselves into very homely places with resident housemothers and housefathers caring for small groups of children. Bowlby however, instead of taking all these earlier factors into account – the uniformed nurses, the rows of unattended cots, the drabness of the environment and the absence of loving care – attributed all the backwardness and emotional deficiencies of these children to the absence of their mothers. As many writers have pointed out, what Bowlby was studying was not the effects of maternal deprivation but the effects of *institutionalisation*.

What seems never to have occurred to Bowlby was that these children were deprived of their homes, their fathers, their siblings and, very frequently, affection. Similarly, Bowlby pays scant attention to the reasons why these children were in institutions in the first place – death of parents, break-up of the home or simply not being wanted by anyone – none of which are conducive to the child's healthy development. But Bowlby refuses to take these factors into account. The only one he does anticipate is the one least likely to be thought of, that is, that the children he observed in institutions may have come from "poor stock, physically and mentally", so that heredity alone might account for their backward development. He tries to refute this (as though the idea in itself were acceptable) with devastating logic, by citing the case of twin goats, one of which was separated from its mother and became "psychologically frozen" when lights were flashed on and off. He concludes this with the following statement:

‘This is ample demonstration of the adverse effects of maternal deprivation on the mammalian young, and disposes finally of the argument that all the observed effects are due to heredity.’

Bowlby's single-minded pursuit of the mother as the villain of the piece often blinds him to his own evidence.

‘Nearly twenty years ago Daniels studied two groups of two-year-olds living in the same institution. "One group was given very little tenderness although adequately cared for in every other respect," while in the other "a nurse was assigned to each child and there was no lack of tenderness and affection. At the end of half a year the first group was mentally and physically retarded, in comparison with the second".’

(We must wonder about the ethics of such conscious and deliberate neglect of children as was practised in this experiment in the pursuit of 'science'.) Now Bowlby refers to this experiment as "positive evidence that the causative factor is maternal deprivation", whereas it merely shows what truly is common sense, that is that children respond and thrive when given loving care and attention. Again one wonders at the mentality of psychiatrists. After six months of deliberate neglect wouldn't Bowlby himself be somewhat "retarded" having received neither warmth nor affection and having only his physical needs met?

In the following instance, Bowlby cited evidence which positively disproves his case:

> ❜Simonsen compared a group of 113 children aged between one and four years almost all of whom had spent their whole lives in one of some 12 different institutions, with a comparable group who lived at home and attended day nurseries. The mothers of these children were working and the homes often very unsatisfactory. Even so, the average developmental quotient of the family children was normal – 102 – while that of the institution children retarded – 93.❜

In a paper designed to stress the adverse effects of maternal deprivation, partial or total, he makes no attempt to account for the healthy development of the day nursery children who were deprived of their mothers for eight or more hours a day. Here, especially, he demonstrated that he is studying the effects of institutionalisation and not maternal deprivation.

Never for a moment does Bowlby shift his attention from the mother. The point is repeated over and over again in his work with phrases like "when deprived of maternal care, the child's development is almost always retarded, physically, intellectually and socially", such children "are gravely damaged for life . . . deprivation of mother love can have far-reaching effects on the mental health and personality development of human beings". There is an unswerving emphasis, not on the fact that children need loving care but that they need their *mothers'* loving care. No-one else's will do. If the parents choose to leave the care of their children with someone else at any time, that person is not uncle, aunt or friend, but mother *substitute*. Bowlby denies grandparents, aunts, older siblings, friends or neighbours the independent right to care for children. Fathers even fall into the same category. In all the lay and professional publications of the Tavistock Institute (where Bowlby is a consultant) fathers are referred to as "occasional substitute *mothers.*"

This confusion between the child's need for love and the assumption that such love can only emanate from the mother reigns as supreme today as it did when Bowlby published his work. Twenty years later the *Sunday Times* can say:

> ❮Mothers have every reason for fearing that even a brief separation from a toddler may, if ill managed, lead to behaviour problems for months afterwards. Tantrums, a break down of toilet training, and moodiness are just some symptoms of the underlying insecurity, and behaviour problems are sometimes so serious after a separation that family life is completely disrupted.❯[1]

Later, in the same article, we are informed that "substitute care" in the form of nannies and au pairs results in "aggressive, anti-social personalities or people highly defended against feelings but vulnerable and unhappy underneath. At the extreme such situations can mould isolated anti-social people and perhaps incipient psychopaths." According to this article, this all apparently happens when the mother spends a few days away in hospital having a baby. It isn't enough to warn mothers that leaving their children in another's care may cause irreparable damage. Bowlby's alarmism in 1947 that separation from the mother caused "delinquent character development" still sways subsequent writers on the subject, only now such children are more fashionably described as "incipient psychopaths". Mothers beware!

It's your responsibility to ensure that the next generation is not a race of psychopathic delinquents.

In the same vein, wide publicity was given to the statements made by Dr. Marie Meirehofer at a Health International Conference in 1972. Her research was done with institutionalised children in Switzerland and, like Bowlby, she attributes their backwardness, speech difficulties and withdrawal symptoms, not to the absence of affection, nor to their institutionalised way of life, nor to the reasons why they are there, but to the absence of their mothers. She asserts that children who attend day nurseries and creches "could have their mental development impaired" and that "an acute deprivation syndrome can quickly be set up when a baby does not receive continual maternal care." She demands that "a weekly wage should be paid to encourage mothers to follow their maternal profession"[2] in order to prevent them from going out to work.

But what about the relationship between working mothers and 'delinquency'? It is an emotive subject and one which prompts many people to put pen to paper to write irate and ill-informed letters which are seriously received in the press and on the radio; because there is little sympathy for young people who demonstrate their frustration and disillusion against a society which brands them, at eleven years old, as 'failures' and which condemns them to a lifetime of boring, mindless work. Evelyn Sullerot, in her sociological study of women, wrote:

‹It seems that the working mother suffers more than her children, despite all that has been said on the subject. The children of working mothers do not have higher rates of sickness, or lower rates of development,

154

they are no worse adjusted (on the contrary they compare favourably) and no more delinquent, despite the tissue of lies that one reads, than the children of mothers who remain at home. On many of these points one can even cite evidence to show that children of working mothers do better than those of non-working mothers, although a copious literature seeks, *without any substantiation*, to designate such children as martyrs.❜ (my emphasis).

The "tissue of lies" gained much currency with the publication of a study called 'Working Mothers and Delinquency' by Glueck and Glueck, a study which actually took as its starting point the assumption that mothers should not go out to work. It is significant that the ripples made by the Gluecks' work extended far beyond the academic circles of social science. The conclusions the Gluecks reached quickly filtered through and became popularly known 'facts'. But a closer look at this famous study reveals exactly how social science is manipulated to deceive the outside world, and directly in this case, oppress women.

The subject of the study was 500 'delinquent' boys, matched pair by pair with non-delinquent boys of similar age and cultural background. The employed mothers were divided into two groups, those regularly employed and those sporadically employed, in similar types of work (cleaning, shop work etc.). Of the delinquent boys 54% had mothers who were full time housewives, compared with 46% whose mothers worked, so a slightly higher proportion of the delinquent boys had full time mothers. When the authors turned to the sporadically employed mothers, many of whom had themselves been delinquents and whose husbands were frequently unemployed, and where both parents were lacking in "self respect", they found a higher proportion of delinquents. Intent on proving that working mothers are the sole cause of delinquency, the authors disregard the other potent factors which contribute to the waywardness of these children and conclude:

‘We already have sufficient evidence to permit of at least a guarded conclusion that the villain among working mothers is the one who seems to have some inner need to flit erratically from job to job probably because she finds relief thereby from the burden of homemaking.’

Note that there is no mention that this "inner need" might be financial, owing to the husband's unemployment, and also that all mothers who work are "villains" who evade their domestic duties. In their conclusion, the authors drop their guard to reveal the moralising assumptions and arrogant prejudice which motivates their 'research':

‘As more and more enticements in the way of financial gain, excitement and independence from the husband are offered married women to lure them from their domestic duties, the problem is becoming more widespread and acute.’

So there it is for all to see – the devil in disguise "luring" and "enticing" women away from homemaking with promises of riches so that they can "flit" from "excitement" to "independence". In fact, as the study painfully shows, these women are desperately poor and wretched and are forced to clean other people's floors for a pittance so that they can pay for their children's food and clothes. The connection between their employment and delinquency is arrant nonsense. Besides the other factors at work in these families, the authors studiously ignore the fact that the fathers were also sporadically employed. Despite the myopia of the Gluecks, their 'findings' continue to provide respectable ammunition for all those people who object to mothers going out to work.

Many of the studies into the effects of maternal employment on children suffer from the same bias. Margaret Broughton in her paper *Children with Mothers at Work* suggested, with incredible naivety:

> '. . . for mothers who work because they are bored or lonely probably the answer would be to provide creches or day nurseries where mothers could leave their children for a few hours so that they could take part-time jobs. An occasional morning or afternoon would probably keep many women mentally happy.'

Which all leaves a picture of women as dogs on leashes who should be allowed an occasional morning run round the park in order to keep them mute and house-trained for the rest of the time.

No single study has been able to prove that delinquency can be attributed to working mothers. In fact, as mentioned previously, the Gluecks found a higher proportion of delinquents from homes where there were full time mothers. So also did Ferguson and Cunnison in their study of delinquents in Glasgow. In an exhaustive review of all the published evidence on the effects of maternal employment on children, Lois Stolz had this to say:

> 'The studies reviewed tend to deny the contention that children of working mothers are more likely to be

delinquent than children of mothers who remain at home.'

In 1965 Warren & Palmer looked into the backgrounds of 316 juvenile offenders and found a staggering 98% without a father figure compared with 17% who lacked a mother. As one social scientist pointed out,

'Paternal deprivation can no more be seen in isolation than the maternal variety.'[3]

It is patently obvious that no study of 'delinquency' can be undertaken without full regard of all the factors – economic, social and educational – which together contribute to the child's development. But these factors are ignored and the popular image of working mothers, 'latch key children' and consequent delinquency still dominates official and lay opinion. Women have been used as scapegoats for far too many of society's ills. Delinquency, as it is understood and persistently mis-represented, is just one of these ills in a long and repetitive cycle of mother-blaming, which succeeds in grinding women down and curtailing their aspirations through guilt so that they can bear the yoke of society's failings more comfortably.

In almost all the studies there is an implicit assumption that maternal employment and maternal neglect are synonymous. Of course, there's no connection, just as there's no connection between maternal presence and what Professor Yudkin calls 'loving attention.' It hardly seems worth saying that the harassed mother who stays at home only out of a sense of duty to her children is as much of a threat to their well being as the mother who reluctantly goes out to work and is

158

frustrated in her job. If the investigators want seriously to continue in this field, they might try assessing the effects on the children of the unhappy full time housewife versus the satisfied working mother. Another area for research might also be the effects of *fathers* going out to work. Such a study might yield very interesting results but as the function of most studies is to confirm existing ideologies, a study on the effects of paternal employment would never be financed.

Despite all these points, the doubt will still linger that the mother who works outside the home, particularly while her children are small, is causing them irreparable damage. Very few studies have been undertaken on the effects of maternal employment on the under fives, this being on the mistaken assumption that women with young children do not go out to work. During the war, many more children attended day nurseries than today, and a group of these children were investigated in a study by Netta Glass. This is one of the few studies which used a control group who were cared for at home rather than an institutionalised group. Unlike other studies, the author investigated home environmental factors, personality and attitudes of the mother and marital situation. When she studied the habit disturbances of the children, she found that 29 of the at-home children were affected compared with 33 of the day nursery children. (The difference, she states, is not statistically significant.) The author noted that the mothers of the day nursery children who presented problems themselves had "difficult personalities", fathers were more frequently absent among the nursery children and living conditions were generally worse. The study illustrated very clearly that the 'problem children' were associated with certain parental attitudes and home situation and not with whether the children did or did not attend day nursery. She concluded that:

‘There was no evidence to suggest that children cared for in a day nursery are more likely by reason of communal care to present developmental problems than are children cared for at home by their mothers.’

A study undertaken by Perry in 1961 in Washington dealt with children aged three to five years of 104 employed mothers. These children were cared for during their mothers' absence by relatives, trained child minders and so on. The children's adjustment, as measured by nervous symptoms, anti-social and withdrawing tendencies showed no correlation with any of these factors and Perry concludes that:

‘. . . results failed to support the views of those who oppose the separation of children from their mothers.’

The emphasis in all these studies is always biased towards the possible harmful effects of partial separation of children from their mothers. I would have been very relieved to have found some research which set out to investigate the *benefits* of communal care for small children. No less important would be a study of the effects of maternal over-protection which ought to prove as interesting as one on the effects of working fathers. Myrdal and Klein noted that over-protection can be as serious as neglect and, like severe neglect, may "cripple the psychological development of the child."

But in the present climate of opinion, no scientist would tarnish the image of boundless mother love with a study of its crippling effects. Concessions are gradually being made towards the provision of nursery school places for 'deprived' children but no-one in authority has yet reconciled the idea that separation from the mother is beneficial to the under-privileged child but harmful to the 'normal' child.*

There is one large and important exception to the general scientific rule I have indicated. In 1972 Michael Rutter published his book 'Maternal Deprivation Re-assessed'. He showed that there was a mountain of published *but unpublicised* research which had not taken, as its starting point, the assumption that separation of children from their mothers was automatically harmful. His book contains findings from over 300 studies under-taken over the last two or three decades which, taken together, substantiate the view that current attitudes to child rearing are based on a mixture of myth and prop-aganda.

Rutter explores at some length the assumption that children can only thrive in hierarchical relationships, with mother at the top descending through father, siblings, grandparents and that the relationship with the mother is the only vital one; an assumption based very securely in the hierarchical nature of the world in which we live. Rutter dispels this myth:

'Schaffer & Emerson (1964) found that the sole principal attachment was to the mother in only half of the 18-month-old children they studied and in nearly a

---

* There are still less than one in ten children under five attending any kind of nursery or pre-school playgroup. Thus nine out of ten children spend their first five years alone in their homes with their mothers (although some are cared for by child minders while their mothers work). The projected plans for nursery expansion are no more than a drop in the ocean. At best, it will only touch four year olds and will give them the opportunity only for half time nursery school attendance.

third of the cases the main attachment was to the father. . . . Bowlby (1969) has argued that there is a bias for a child to attach himself to *one* figure (a characteristic he has called 'monotropy') and that this main attachment differs in kind from attachments to subsidiary figures. However, there is a lack of supporting evidence for this claim; Schaffer (1971) has concluded that Bowlby's view is not borne out by the facts and that the breadth of attachments is largely *determined by the social setting.*❜ (my emphasis).

The view that the young child needs one constant figure attending to her takes a further battering. Having reviewed the evidence from all the studies, Rutter states:

❛It may be concluded that it is *not* necessary for mothering to be provided by only one person . . . if mothering is of high quality and is provided by figures who remain the same during the child's early life then (at least up to four or five mother-figures) multiple mothering need have no adverse effects.❜

The use of the term 'mothering' here is slightly misleading, but elsewhere in the book, Rutter defines it as a quality not specific to mothers or, indeed, to women, but as a combination of "warmth and stimulating interaction". On this subject, he brings together a wealth of evidence to show that the childs deepest attachment is not dependent on the person he or she spends most time with. Because mothers take on the bulk of the physical care of small children and spend more time with them than other members of the family, we have assumed that the child will be more dependent on the mother's love than on anyone else's. What Rutter shows – and in retrospect it seems ridiculously obvious – is that the child's attachments are determined by the *intensity* of the relationship rather than its duration. In other words, it is the person(s) the child plays with, talks with and learns from (and this may be the mother) who is more important than the person who attends to his physical needs. So often, it is fathers, siblings and grandparents (whose affection for the children is not marred by concerns with the running of the home and the care of other children and adults) who can give the young child their undivided attention and who have the time to play and talk with her far more constructively than the mother. And these are the people to whom the child will be attached.

A lot of attention has been focused on the separation of children from their mothers when they (the children) have to go to hospital. There are a number of films on the schools and charity organisations circuit which purport to show that the sometimes heartrending consequences of hospitalization on young children are entirely due to the separation of the child from his mother. The result has been the mushrooming of pressure groups who are persuading hospitals to allow mothers to stay with their children. Rutter shows, what again seems obvious, that the child's distress is due to the strange and often frightening environment. The effects on children can be softened by the presence of a familiar person but there is not a shred of evidence to show that it must be the mother.

Rutter also refers to a great deal of work which has been done on Bowlby's dictum that "a bad home is preferable to a good institution" and shows that this is "obvious nonsense" and "scarcely warrants consideration" and he notes with regret the reluctance of child care authorities to remove children "from even appalling home circumstances".

In the conclusion to his book, in sharp contrast to the sensationalism and scare-mongering of scientists who have the ear of the public and having carefully assessed all the published evidence to date, he notes:

> ‘Two issues are involved. The first is whether the main bond differs from all the others. It is suggested here that it does not . . . most children develop bonds with several people and it appears likely that these bonds are basically similar. The second concerns the assumption that the ‘mother’ or ‘mother surrogate’ is the person to whom the child is necessarily most attached. Of course in most families the mother has most to do with the young child and as a consequence she is usually the person with whom the strongest bond is formed. But it should be appreciated that the chief bond need not be with a biological parent, it need not be with the chief caretaker and it need not be with a female.’

Thus we can no longer impose as ‘natural’ on our children a need to be cared for solely by their mothers, simply because this suits the demands of our economic system.

* * * * * * *

Childbirth and the Mystique of Motherhood

NOT only is the child supposed to need her mother's exclusive care and attention but the mother is, in turn, the only person fitted to give it. And that, in turn, is what femininity, as it has come to be understood, is often about.

> ‘Mothering, in short, is not simply one of the things women do. It is the activity that, above all, completes and confirms feminine identity.’[1]

So all the women in history who did not regard motherhood as the supreme affirmation of their identities, who shared the care of their children with others and who devoted their time and energy to other things, and all women today who, whether or not they have children, find their primary role outside motherhood and who, like men, regard having children as just one of the things people do, must be condemned as having incomplete and inadequate identities. And the millions of women in the poor countries of the world, who work all their lives and regard child bearing as just one of their many functions in the community, must also be condemned for denying their raison d'etre.

What we can see is that the ideology of the child's emotional dependency on the mother had to give rise to the converse. If the child can only be made complete by the mother dancing constant attendance, then the woman can only be made complete by attending to the child. We would otherwise have a situation where women's servitude to children was evidently unjust. Their willingness to serve the child must be encouraged on the basis that such action is not self-denial but self-enhancement.

Like the prevailing ideas about child care, the assumption that women can only realise their ultimate identities through having and caring for a child – what I shall call the mystique of motherhood – is a very recent phenomenon. It is, as Margaret Mead has perceptively stated, "a new and subtle form of anti-feminism"[2] and it could only come to fruition in a society which is anti-women.

Throughout history and throughout the non-industrial parts of the world now, there has been and is no such mystique. When women must be occupied with tilling the fields, tending the crops and domestic animals and weaving cloth, when the very youngest children are strapped onto people's backs while the adults work alongside the older children, then motherhood cannot be set aside in a special fulfilling category, debarring women from any other ticket to adulthood. Similarly, in our own society, only fifty or so years ago, as we saw in the previous chapter, women worked long, productive hours both in and out of the home; so motherhood could not be elevated and singled out as women's only destiny, just as it would have been literally incomprehensible to the people of the Middle Ages. There is much evidence, gathered together in Philip Aries' book, 'Centuries of Childhood', to indicate that children were not then regarded as a separate sub-species of humanity requiring special treatment. Because society was not then divided up into small family units, as soon as children could walk they lived and worked alongside adults. Instead of being hived off to separate living and sleeping quarters and being tolerated until they reached what we define as adulthood, their role and place in the community was as a functioning part of that community. Commenting on Aries' book, Gathorne Hardy notes:

'Households of this period, and on into Stuart times,

166

were enormous. A household of sixty was not considered large. They were composed, apart from servants (who did not have the lowly status they have today) of the ramifications of entire families; uncles, aunts, grandparents, in-laws and cousins. But these families weren't considered as units for producing and bringing up children, as they are today; they were considered as a line, a dynasty, a group related by blood and marriage. . . . A family was an economic and defensive/offensive unit – like the village, the manor, the castle. Children were not important to this sort of family, nor was the family important to the children. Other units – peer group units, servant units – were of far more consequence to children.**'** (my parenthesis).

There is one other factor to consider and that is that no mystique of motherhood could flourish when perhaps only half the children born to women would survive and when childbirth itself was a common cause of women's death.

It is only when women are considered largely useless – when their economic role as producers is appropriated by men and when women's *presence* in the home is valued more highly than their labour in it, that motherhood can emerge as a peg on which to hang half the human race. Freud said of women that "Anatomy is destiny" but that can only be so when women are denied any other destiny.

And so women have come to be regarded, judging from the propaganda, as victims of their hormones, ever susceptible to the remorseless cycle of menarche, menstruation, pregnancy, childbirth, recuperation, menstruation, menopause and obsolescence. Overlaying the whole structure is the notion that:

> ‘A woman's identity is more slowly structured than a man's and more closely related to physiology. A girl's sense of identity is linked to the reproductive process.’[3]

A baby producing machine? Professor Rhodes, in a recent biological study of 'Woman' wrote:

> ‘The problem of the education of girls today is that it is still run by academics who perhaps place too high a premium on academic achievement. About 90% of girls will have children, mainly within the confines of marriage, and for this, academic attainment, however desirable for other reasons, is not necessary, and many girls know it. . . . Perhaps a good reason for keeping the sexes separate in their formal education is to be found in the very great physiological differences in girls and in their vocational and games and play needs.’

There is much to quarrel with Professor Rhodes. Ninety per cent of boys, we must assume, will also have children but do they have to be re-educated to fit them for their adult role? Can their education be dismissed as irrelevant because one day they will be fathers? Professor Rhodes reveals his prejudice in the last sentence quoted where we learn that girls' play and vocational needs are entirely dependent on their biology, on their reproductive function. If our society truly valued women's child bearing function and if it was not regarded as a serious handicap, justifying their exclusion from almost every important sphere of life, then it might be possible to re-write his piece in the following way:

> ‘Perhaps a good reason for keeping the sexes separate

168

in their formal education is to be found in the very great physiological differences in boys and in their vocational and games and play needs, owing to their inability to bear children. 9

We are dealing, very concretely, with the debasement of women. Their child-bearing function is always held up as the ultimate justification for their inferior position in society and that can only come about in a situation where child-bearing is, in itself, devalued. The mystique of motherhood merely disguises an underlying state of affairs in which pregnancy and childbirth are regarded (particularly by the medical world) as blots on an otherwise ordered world. It is significant that the other blot – the ills of old people – are lumped together and frequently the geriatric and maternity departments are placed together in the grimmest and most inaccessible parts of hospitals.

Every woman who has had a baby in these circumstances can testify to the distressing treatment they are subjected to, as though pregnancy were some sort of *disease*. It also seems that once a woman has a child in her body, all brains or ability she ever had are supposed to vanish. She is prodded, poked, told not to be stupid while being treated as a mental defective and whatever she has to say about her condition will be dismissed as the jabberings of a cretin. This sort of treatment is of quite a different order from the usual superior doctor/inferior patient relationship. If the woman in labour asks what they are doing to her, or whether she really needs to be cut or whether they can hear the heart beat, she will as often as not be told 'It's none of your business, dear'. If she says she doesn't want drugs and she's coping quite well with the pain, thank you, they turn her over and say 'We just want to feel you dear' while they jab in the pethidine. When she says she's ready to push now, they say, 'Don't be silly, it's only a feeling.' There is mounting evidence too, that the baby's inclination to be born when it's ready, at any time of day or night, is a further nuisance that must be eradicated. There is a growing practice called 'daylight obstetrics' where the pregnant woman is admitted into hospital when *they* think the child is due, labour is induced early in the morning so that the babies will be born by tea time. The obstetrician can then go home and have a round of golf before dinner.

I spent a week in an ante-natal ward of a perfectly average maternity hospital and talked with all the women there. I have talked also with many other women about their experiences of childbirth in hospital and read many accounts which, together with my own experience, has convinced me that being treated by the medical staff as a mindless vehicle of reproduction is far more traumatic than the birth itself. The tragedy is that so many women are philosophical about it and cannot imagine things being any different.

The following two cases are known to me personally and most mothers have their own testimony in addition to those experienced by other women with whom they were in hospital. These are telling accounts of the devaluation of childbirth which women have suffered and learnt from and which cannot be dismissed, comfortably, as 'old wives' tales', 'childbirth horror stories' or 'women's gossip'. It is time women were heard seriously.

Dorigen, who told the staff when she went into labour that she was allergic to pethidine. She was told not to interfere – they knew best – and was injected with it, despite her protestations. She spent the ten hours of her labour vomiting.

Mrs. J. (whom I met in hospital) was under intensive care for high blood pressure in the ante-natal ward. She had two sons and had been trying for five years to have a girl but had miscarried twice. She was 8 months pregnant when she started labour but was given the 'Don't-be-silly-dear' routine, 'You've got four weeks to go.' Hours later, in the early hours of the morning, she insisted that she was giving birth. The sister in charge refused to wake the doctor, even though complications had been expected. By the time they finally believed her, she was well into the second stage of labour and she gave birth to what they knew was a breech baby while being rushed down from the ante-natal ward to the labour ward. She suffered terribly and the baby died three hours later. The medical staff admitted later that it was an obvious case for a Caesarean. When she left the hospital she was told 'Never mind, you can try again'. She was 38 years old and a year later adopted a girl, after having had herself sterilised.

Cases like these are not isolated instances. They happen every day in maternity hospitals and account for the increasing tendency, circumstances allowing, for women to have their second babies at home. At least there, they are safe from the cattle market procedure with the vet (obstetrician) talking to the farmer (midwife) about the possibility of this specimen producing twins, as though, like a cow, the woman was a deaf mute, indifferent to her and her children's fate.

Despite the attempts of the magazines and baby books to raise women's spirits by telling them that pregnancy gives them 'a new bloom of beauty' and that it is a 'wonderful maturing experience' (are childless women immature?) and that the minor discomforts of pregnancy are outweighed by the special regard in which they are held by their family, nothing can disguise the fact that pregnancy, in this society, is regarded as a nuisance. Employers and the medical profession regard women's child bearing function as something which *interferes* with the normal course of events. They would perhaps be happier if we were all immortal, so that this irritating tendency of women to have babies from time to time could be done away with.

The nuisance element is further intensified by the advice given to men in their dealings with their pregnant wives. They are told that their wives might be emotional, that they may fly off the handle and burst into tears but not to worry because it's just their hormones. As the hormones released during pregnancy are exactly those of the contraceptive pill, one might reasonably ask whether the tearfulness of pregnant women might not have other causes. What is certain is that the pregnant woman frequently comes face to face with the truth underlying the mystique. She walks down the street and has to face the ribald and sometimes plainly offensive comments of men ("And what were you doing last Christmas?" or "Haven't you had it for a bit then?"). And the special regard of her family is not always welcome when it means being treated like a vessel whose cargo is more valuable than the vessel itself. And when she goes to hospital for the first ante-natal check, riding on the waves of blossoming womanhood which the mystique engendered only to have it all swept away by the contempt which it disguises, is it not surprising that she bursts into tears when she comes home and is it not surprising, as the books fondly tell us, that the pregnant woman 'turns in on herself'?

The fatuous ideas about pregnancy are given their full weight in quite respectable sources. Thus Professor

Rhodes attributes the tendency of women to go in for house cleaning and home-making to their hormones and smugly suggests that it is exactly like the nest-building instinct in birds. No mention that, having given up going to work in the last weeks of pregnancy and finding herself, probably for the first time in her life, with free time on her hands, that it might be a sensible idea to clean the place up and prepare a room for the child. No, no, it can't be that. Because women aren't rational beings like men. They are just victims of their reproductive function, driven by their instinctual and hormonal drives which mark them out as a lower form of life.

The State's attitude to pregnancy and childbirth confirms society's hypocrisy. Evelyn Sullerot surveyed the attitudes of the member countries of the OECD to maternity leave and payments. The 1952 Convention fixes minimal standards which include "six weeks compulsory leave after childbirth and six weeks optional leave before the expected date of delivery, as well as security of tenure for pregnant women and payment of allowances during their leave". These twenty-one countries represent the 'advanced' nations of the world and yet only seven even signed the Convention. Sullerot also notes that even those few do not put their good intentions into practice and none fulfils even the Convention's minimum standards. Sweden, Yugoslavia and France make the best provision but it is significant that those are also just the countries which are concerned about their low birth rate and where women's child bearing function changes from being a private problem to a social activity.

The mystique of motherhood can be maintained by pointing to women's 'natural' maternal instincts, as though there were some biological link between bearing children and washing nappies. It is also supposed to endow the woman with the ability to care for even a large brood of children single handed. But worse is the belief that our instincts are naturally privatized, that the love and protection we extend to our biological children is of a different and altogether deeper order than our love for all children. Again, this has come about because we live in a privatized/ownership world and we seek justification of it by attributing it to our instincts. As any parent who has fostered or adopted children can say, love grows through knowing and caring for a child and not from any biological link. These parents' grief when their children are taken from them and returned to their natural parents would be no different were the children their 'own'.

It has been pointed out that one of the most fundamental (not just female) qualities is the immediate response to a helpless being. Think of young children watching nature films and all sighing 'aaah' when a baby animal appears. But at the critical age when boys are being taught to assert their masculinity and drop their childish (female) ways, they struggle desperately to suppress this response so that by the time they've grown up, they've forgotten they ever had it. One of the great strengths of women is that, unlike men, their tendency to respond to babies, small animals, the sick and the old with care and affection has not been wholly distorted. The pressure on men to fulfil acceptable expectations of masculinity and to detach themselves from 'female' qualities has resulted in the state of affairs which we are trained to regard as normal. The parental instinct has become a maternal instinct, which virtually exempts men from the care of children altogether and which asserts that women can only love their biological offspring.

In fact, as many women have discovered but are afraid openly to admit, the hoped-for uprush of maternal feelings, as soon as their first baby is put into their arms, does not automatically materialise. It has to be worked for. There are good reasons for this. Society is strictly segregated into age groups and unless one comes from a large and well spaced out family, women come to child-birth without previous knowledge or experience of babies; in this respect they are no different from men. But both men and women are brought up to believe that the presence of a womb is the automatic guarantee of maternal instincts. (Many men will be surprised to learn that they too have wombs, albeit vestigial and hard to find.) It is rather like suggesting that if a male office bound clerk were uprooted and placed in the middle of an African jungle, he would straightaway revert to his 'animal' instincts and know how to hunt. Despite misty-eyed, male, wishfulfilling talk of women's maternal drive, young childless women are no more knowledgeable in baby care than are men.

We must pity men their deep loss in substituting 'masculine' behaviour for 'feminine' behaviour; that is, the capacity to give, without thought of return, a capacity which finds its direct expression in child care. For women relearn, through child care, what men perpetually un-learn and often deny. The human capacity to love and care for the young has been horribly distorted; if that capacity could be quantified, which thankfully it can't, then we could see that it has been taken from the male half of the race and that the female half has had its share *doubled*.

Margaret Mead commented very perceptively on the separation of men from small children. At the third meeting of the World Health Organisation Study Group on Child Development, she said:

‘In very simple societies, such as the Australian Aborigines, many South Sea island societies, and some African societies, the male takes a great deal of care of the young infant. But with every society that we have any record of, with the onset of what you call civilisation, division of labour, class structure, hierarchies of authority etc., one of the first things that has happened has been the separation of the human male from his own baby until any point up to two years, four years, six years, twelve years. I think one of the things we may want to discuss here is whether this is not a *condition* of civilization.’

Not only are men denied an equal share in the rearing of children in Western society but divisions are erected between the women who take on, in addition to their own, the responsibility that men have relinquished. Instead of the women being allowed to share out the work between them as they have always done in the past and continue to do in the poor countries, it is now off-loaded onto the individual biological mother. So the spectacle of the young woman today, caring in isolation for two, three or four children all day without help and without the chance to do anything else has come to be regarded as normal and desirable. The Aborigine that Mead speaks of might rightly suspect us of being a very strange race of people, subjecting women and children to such an incredibly distorted state of affairs. He might rightly wonder how a society can hive women and children off and define itself by their exclusion.

But to protect itself against the charge of in-humanity, the ideology points to the woman at home, battling with the continuous and conflicting needs of a toddler and a four year old in an environment exclusively designed for adults, and wraps up her situation in rose-

176

coloured tissue paper and ties it with a bow labelled 'creativity'. There she is, fulfilling all her creative potential, exercising her raison d'etre, and acting as a convenient repository for the values we all cherish but would prefer not to know about so we sweep them away under the carpet of society into the home.

Society's attitude to small children is hypocritical in the extreme. The acknowledgment that having children is not roses all the way is extended to everyone except the person most concerned – the mother who takes on 24 hour responsibility. Children are not welcome anywhere. Like dogs, they are only tolerated if they're on a lead. Libraries, cafes, department stores, pubs and adult education classes are all forbidden places if you have an averagely lively, energetic, noisy and curious three year old.

The harassed mother is a very real phenomenon. There is no similar large scale male experience to the depths of desperation which every mother sinks to, having dragged, pushed and carried an alternatively boisterous and recalcitrant small child up and down escalators, on and off buses, in and out of shops and whose only recognition is the odd benign smile from an old person and a sea of disapproving, condemnatory and hostile glances. ("Why won't she keep her children in *order*.") A woman does only have two hands and the brutality I have been subjected to by shopkeepers, having put down my 20 lb. bag of shopping and let go of my child to fumble in my purse for change, in the space of which time she makes a grab for a bar of chocolate (deliberately placed at child level) and tips up the whole display, must be experienced to be understood.

In fact, the only place where children are welcome

is school (and circuses and fairs where their parents' money is actually more welcome than the children). A group of women who had children of varying ages discussed their experiences at a women's meeting. One woman said she had had to stop taking her four year old to the park (two bus rides away) because he had been told once too often to keep off the grass. Another woman had been horrified by being asked to leave a *toy* shop. Her child had actually played with the toys on display and annoyed the manager. Travelling on public transport with children is a nightmare. My own town, along with many others in Britain, has introduced one man operated buses in the name of efficiency. The absence of the conductor only penalises those who are less than able-bodied, that is mothers with push chairs, young children, the handicapped and the old. Thus, another member of the group, eight months pregnant at the time, had given up going into the market in town, not because she felt unfit but because she'd been very distressed by humping her two year old onto the bus, going back to fold up the push-chair and shove that on and then going back for her shopping bags and then paying her fare to the driver and being told by him "Hurry up lady, I've got a schedule to keep" and the impatient reluctance of the other passengers to regard her as anything but a visitor from another planet. (It is significant that the only people who hold doors open for women with children are other women who know what it's about. As many women now know, the supposed gallantry of men towards women, the little gestures and so on, cease abruptly when that woman is patently not available – viz. small child.)

This is an anti-child society and anyone who thinks otherwise either hasn't had children or has been duped by the pretty baked bean fed children on television. Children can only be regarded as a nuisance, as a threat to marriages (e.g. the many articles in the media with titles like 'How not to let your baby spoil your marriage'), as a drain on resources and as a restriction on parents' freedom in a society which, physically and psychologically, excludes children. Society, by definition is adult and has spending power.

Judging from the prevailing mystique, however, children are not a nuisance, they are not demanding or exhausting so long, that is, as they are kept where they are supposed to belong – at home with their mothers or firmly locked up in school. And if there is even a murmur of resistance from the mothers, they are told that their maternal instincts will carry them through and that they've got the best years of their children's lives to see to and what could be more important than bringing up the next generation? We might ask that if bringing up children is really considered as important as the propaganda says, and if it is so creative and fulfilling, why is it that men are so reluctant to do it?

Men may joke about it but the reality is very different. I asked all the housewives I interviewed whether their husbands would be prepared to change places with them and stay home to look after the children while the women went out to work (on the imaginary assumption that the women could bring home the same amount of money as their husbands). *Not one* believed that their husbands would stand it. Many of their husbands had, in fact, stayed at home to look after the youngest while their wives had their second or third babies and they had talked about their experiences with their wives. These women said that their men were far more sympathetic about the amount of work involved and had stopped making remarks like 'You have it easy here at home while I slog my guts out at work'. On the question of a more

179

permanent change in roles, the women were adamant. Thus, a typical comment was:

> ‘He'd hate it. I suppose if it came to it, he'd be able to cope but he'd be desperate to get back to work. He says "You're doing the same thing all the time" and when I said "So are you at work", he said that was different!’

Another said:

> ‘He had Darren and Julie once when I was ill for a fortnight, and he said he didn't know how I managed all the time. He wouldn't hear of changing places. Oh no.’

Though she has little choice in the matter, we have to recognise that the willingness of women to sacrifice their jobs, their income and many of their interests in order to devote themselves to the full time, unaided care of their children is nothing less than *heroic*. Because – and this will never find its way into the popular literature on child care – the result of one person taking sole charge of children is that the pleasure of caring for them, watching them grow, protecting them and teaching them is largely outweighed by the day to day frustrations, the restrictions imposed by the outside world and the enormous amount of physical work. None of the stresses of child care are supposed to make inroads into the expression of her identity that motherhood is supposed to constitute. To the sheer physical pressures on the woman must be added her fear of disapproval if she suggests that though she loves her children very much, she really doesn't enjoy their undiluted company *every minute of every day*.

To other people, small children are a 'mixed blessing', while to her they are supposed to be 'pure joy'.

180

But the joy is fleeting. It has to be snatched where it can, clung on to and remembered lest it gets submerged beneath the nappies, the sleepless nights, the potties, the worn-out shoes, the fights, the tantrums and the rivalry, which are the consequences of childhood as it is treated and understood. (Some of these features of childhood seem normal to us but are quite unheard of in other societies.) What mothers have to do – and they do it astonishingly well – is to present to their families and to the outside world, a smiling face, a face which colludes with the public's hypocrisy and maintains that mother-hood is one long succession of fulfilling moments – the baby's first smile, step or word, its triumph over the potty, its eagerness to discover the world, its unexpected displays of affection and generosity and its poignant vulnerability. But these are the occasional *perks* of motherhood – it's like suggesting that a frustrating job in a factory is made worthwhile by the odd fringe benefits, as though the man works all the year round just for the bonus in his Christmas pay packet.

Significantly, women are forced to maintain this collusion with each other. The taboo on their economic dependence is matched by the taboo on their experience as mothers. They may be able to share the odd grumble between each other about being tired and overworked, but they cannot speak of their desperation. They cannot talk about what being cooped up all day with their children does to them (and, of course to their children), nor can they speak of the precarious ambivalence of their situation – of the sometimes overwhelming love they feel for their children which has to vie with their feelings of violence. The difficulties of their situation are tailor-made to breed resentment which is made all the more intoler-able by the social pressure not to give way to it. Who can really wonder at the woman who does give way – but all we do is put the battered baby in a hospital and the mother in prison or mental home. And so, also, they cannot speak of what has been called the 'infantilization' process, a process which often renders them incapable of sustaining an adult conversation, so accustomed are they, day in and day out, to a two and three year old level of communication. Mothers cannot speak seriously of these things to each other because their relations with other women are conducted across divisions which society sets up between them, divisions which are propped up by the lies about the fulfilment and creativity of motherhood.

The woman who has felt close to chucking her screaming baby through the window and jumping out after it herself is eaten with guilt and convinced that something is dreadfully wrong with her. The woman whose patience with her three year old's tantrums is exhausted (tantrums often brought about by the impossibility of explaining to children "why they cannot have what television has told them they cannot live without")[4] understands only too well why other mothers leave their children. The woman who does not face each day with a beatific smile and who knows that the joys of motherhood are mostly mindless explanations of why water comes out of a tap and why the child can't have another ice cream when the musical van comes round for the third time in one day, and who cannot let her young child out to play because there is no garden and only a busy main road, is constrained to silence. And the woman who, though she might have had an interesting job, chose to give it up in order to have two children close together like everyone else but who, after seven years of doing nothing but caring for them, feels she's been deprived of her adulthood. She cannot speak seriously of her unhappiness because she thinks she *chose* it. So she, too, is mute.

It is in these and many other ways that the mystique of motherhood remains intact – the fantasy ever untarnished by the reality. Motherhood is the best kept secret in the universe and it is women who have to keep it; they cannot tell it because to do so is to break the chain on which the whole of society depends. They are like flies caught in a web of society's making, each one locked in her own consciousness which tells her that others are free and that her hell is her private problem which she must cope with by pretending that it doesn't exist.

If we add to that hell the confusions which surround the subject and the conflicting pressures on women not only to be mothers, but to be *good* mothers, then we can begin to understand how it is that women who have gone through this tunnel emerge at the other end as a caricature of everything that men believe about women. They are 'neurotic', resentful of male privilege and freedom, passive in big decisions but bossy in small ones, scatterbrained (try spoon feeding a baby and read the newspaper at the same time and remember what you've read), inadequate in public life, gossipy and emotionally labile.

Not surprisingly, the impossible difficulties of bringing up children single-handed are recognised when, occasionally, it is men who do it. Thus, in a review of the book 'Motherless Families' by George and Wilding, we learn that:

‘Loneliness and depression hit the fathers hard . . . Depression, says the study, is caused by the father's way of life – the loss of income, the domestic burden, the problems of combining work and the care of children, the undivided responsibilities, the never ending succession of days filled with work and evenings and weekends filled with chores.**[5]**

A fact which seems to have escaped the reviewer is that this is an apt description of *every mother's* way of life (whether she is employed or not), but books aren't written about her, crocodile tears are not shed for her loss of freedom and income, and 24 hour never ending responsibility is not a 'domestic burden' but her special privilege.

Similarly, Nicholas Tucker bewails the lot of the unfortunate father. He seems very worried about the intrusion of children into father's ordered and infinitely superior way of life. He wrote:

> Increasingly, though, father is beginning to play a much fuller part within the family. In fact, Uri Bronfennbrenner estimates that now, in the United States, the father on average takes part in more activities with his sons than his wife does. This can sometimes have implications for his career; the scientist, faced with a breakthrough towards the late afternoon in the lab, may be in trouble if it is also his evening for putting the children to bed. There may also be less time for friends after work, or solo visits to the pub or club. Indeed, if he does not live near his work, his friends at home may be made through his wife or even his children.**[6]** (God forbid that he should stoop so *low*!)

Poor father, not being able to go off whenever he pleases, restricted in his friendships, his freedom curtailed and his career at risk. No mention that his wife hasn't even got a lab to go to, that her 'breakthrough' is only a new recipe and that her entire experience of the world stems from her position as *mother*, and not as a person.

The only difference between the men of George and Wilding's book, the men of Tucker's fantasies, and the millions of women everywhere who are sparing men from the conflicts of parenthood, is that society and sociologists pity men when circumstances force them to do 'women's work'. No-one would dare to suggest to a man that bringing up children was creative and fulfilling and *yet the work is the same, whoever does it, male or female.*

Bowlby seems not to have grasped this elementary point. In an interview, he said:

> **‘**I think it's just sour grapes suggesting that there is something wrong with a woman devoting herself entirely to her child.**’**[7]

If men were the child rearers, one might ask whether Bowlby would still think it was "sour grapes" when they complained about their lot, having had to give up jobs and incomes to devote themselves entirely to child care, just so that women remained free to pursue their outside work and interests. And would it be sour grapes if men suggested that though they loved their children, they didn't find feeding them, dressing them, struggling through shops and playing peek-a-boo all day and every day, to the exclusion of anything else, totally satisfying? And would it still be sour grapes if they felt a little resentful of their wives' freedom to enjoy the children's company for a few hours a week without being dragged down by the worry for their health and welfare, and who were able to go off to "pub or club" when they'd had enough, without a second thought. Or would Bowlby and every other man instantly do an about-face and say that no single person, man or woman, should have exclusive responsibility for children?

185

When the mystique of motherhood, which both hides and disguises the reality of the woman at home, is stripped away, we do find that there is something deeply wrong with a woman devoting herself entirely to her child. It is no more healthy for a child to be cooped up all day with one woman (or man) than it is for the woman. But, according to the mystique, only the child may be at risk. The pressure on mothers to deny any self interest has put some women's liberation groups, who are campaigning for more nurseries, into the position where their only line of attack is to stress the benefits of nursery schools for the children. That the woman would thus be freed (only from 9 till 3.30 p.m.) remains best unsaid, for these women have to prove to the satisfaction of their city fathers that their militancy stems not from a desire for a basic human right, but from the dictates of the mystique of motherhood.

* * * * * * *

The New Mother

BABY care, as Elizabeth Janeway points out, used not to be a private affair between parents and children. It went on in public in an atmosphere of general consensus. The tradition of women's knowledge, orally passed down and shared in common sisterhood has been destroyed by modern, male dominated medicine. Unlike their predecessors, women today have to turn to books which filter the experience at third hand and disguise the truth. They come to parenthood fearful, ignorant of their own bodies and inexperienced in child care.

But the legacy of women's knowledge persists and asserts that, once she is at home alone with her newborn baby, her instincts will tell her what to do. (Dr. Spock is particularly good at telling women to fall back on their instincts when his book is no help.) The tragedy is that many women are taken in and dearly anticipate the mystery of babies being revealed to them as soon as they come home from hospital, only to find themselves horribly alone, terrified and ignorant. The realisation – and it is shattering – that a lifetime spent in school, in a shop, factory or office does not endow them with maternal insights is a shock from which it takes a long time to recover. Their feelings of fear and inadequacy – that they ought to know how to soothe a crying baby but don't, their deep and inadmissible suspicion that they do not love the baby in the way they are supposed to, their total lack of confidence ("Is the baby under/over-fed?"), their knowledge that everyone else expects them to know, conspire to make them feel that they are not real women. Thus each new mother is a link in a chain which preserves the mystique and ensures that the secret is never told. She inherits it, keeps it and for her own and everyone else's protection, passes it on.

Some resilient women have attempted, tentatively, to chip away at the secret. Jill Tweedie broke a ten year self-imposed silence when she said:

> ❝Maternity was not for me doing what came naturally. It took me four months to think of my child as anything else than 'a baby' and it was only in the day by day tending of him that love began to grow.❞[1]

Another woman, writing on the break up of her marriage, said:

> ❝When the second child was born (yes, another boy) he didn't breathe at first and I lay there praying that he would die so that I could escape from the whole mess. I refused to touch him and John had to feed him for the first three weeks.❞[2]

It has long been recognised within the darkest recesses of the law, that maternal love is not as automatic nor as universal as the propaganda suggests. A woman may kill her child in the first year of its life and the law will do little about it. It is known that childbirth and baby care take their toll of the woman's mental and physical health, but it is doubtful whether the same leniency would be shown if she did a bit of shoplifting.

In the supposed intimacy of the family, the new mother is at pains to put on a brave face. None of the books she consulted while she was pregnant warned her what it would really be like. She had thought, because no-one had told her otherwise, that she would instantly return to her pre-pregnant state, slim, lively and healthy with no more of the discomforts of pregnancy to contend with. But what happens? She returns from hospital so sore that she can barely sit down in one position for more

188

than a few minutes. She has piles, stitches, constipation, agonisingly tender breasts and she is still enormously fat with acres of loose, spare skin and she finds, probably more demoralising than anything else, that the only clothes she can get into are the maternity smocks she's been wearing for the last three months. And if she's breast feeding, she has to wear what has been described as 'gruesome looking underwear' and, to cap it all, sanitary towels (for six weeks) over genitals which look and feel like a plucked chicken with the re-growth of hair as prickly as crabs.

And any notion that she might return to her lively, active state is immediately squashed by the long awaited product which adamantly refuses to be treated as a pleasant addition to her life. The plans she made in the later stages of pregnancy to do all sorts of things after the baby's birth recede into poignant memories. The books had told her that a newborn baby sleeps for twenty out of the twenty-four hours a day, which paints a lovely picture of hours of free time to do all the things she never had time for when she was a nine to five worker.

‘No-one who hasn't had a small child can understand the homicidal fatigue which builds and builds with lack of sleep, worry, no time to relax or think and the totality of the responsibility for a helpless small life.’[3]

The baby books say, along with midwives and health visitors, that babies only need feeding every four hours and that it should take a maximum of half an hour. But, as many women have said, the babies haven't read the books. My own child, who I've since discovered was by no means unusual, demanded to be fed every three hours and took an hour over it every time. And still she cried. And no-one who hasn't experienced it can know the agony of going to bed at midnight, having fed the baby at eleven and be woken again at two o'clock in the morning and then again at five o'clock, day in and night out for six or more weeks. And those odd hours when the baby does sleep, the poor wretched woman, who has never even been given a chance to recover from childbirth, has to spend her time wading through the mountains of washing which a baby makes. And in all this she has to find time to do all the housework, shopping, cooking and cleaning.

It is very difficult to sleep during the last six weeks of pregnancy. The baby kicks and the sheer size of the woman's body makes it impossible to get into a comfortable position. Sleep in hospital after the birth is out of the question with the constant to-ing and fro-ing of the staff, new births and the effort to identify one's own out of the chorus of babies. By the time the baby is six weeks old the new mother probably hasn't had an uninterrupted night's sleep for well on three months. Add to that her nervousness over her treatment of her child, her uncertainty about its inner workings, the dreadful state of her own body and the different and bewildering way in which her family and friends treat her – as a Mother instead of the person inside that she is trying to salvage from the mess around her – and you have the necessary criteria for a deep depression – 'the post-natal blues'. It will probably not now come as a surprise to learn that the medical world attributes this very common phenomenon not to the woman's situation, not to her blinding fatigue, not to the terrible anti-climax it all is, but to her *hormones*.[4]

Other people are very interested in new babies. They come in and look and peer and ask to hold the baby, they talk about who it looks like and then gingerly hand it back. No-one asks the mother what she is really feeling and if she tries to talk about it, they retreat, embarrassed and shocked. When she says that the baby might look sweet and endearing now but it screams most of the night until she's ready to ring up the NSPCC because she's close to beating it, they either laugh indulgently and say 'Oh, that'll pass soon' or else they go and ring the NSPCC themselves. If she says that she didn't think motherhood meant spending every waking minute when she's so tired she's barely able to see, attending to menial tasks or feeding the baby and that the joy of having given birth to new life is meaningless when she's face to face with a squawling baby who doesn't care who feeds or clothes it so long as it is warm and fed.

It is the totality of the responsibility for a new life which is so overwhelming. Even if the baby is good (i.e. sleeps) she can't enjoy her free time. She has to jump up every ten minutes to check that the child is breathing. Or else the anxiety suppresses itself in a kind of amnesia.

‘She was about a month old and Dave came home from work early one day and it was a gorgeous day and he said "let's go out for a drive". You know we'd gone about 10 miles before we remembered that we'd forgotten her. We raced back and there she was screaming her head off.’

Another woman I interviewed twice went home leaving her baby in its pram outside the local shop. She, too, had simply 'forgotten' she had a baby.

* * * * * * *

The Task of Child Rearing

MORE learning takes place in the first five years of life than any other period of human life. We have only to look at a helpless newborn infant and a five year old child to see that this is true. In those societies which have no need of child care theories because their children are an integral part of the community, the child's capacity to learn through practice, imitation and experience is not atrophied by subjecting the child to the control of one person in isolation from the rest of society. Toys and playthings would be a strange anachronism in cultures where children have no need of miniature fantasy versions of the phenomena of the real world, because those children are not excluded from that world. Thus young children in these societies learn about the world they live in by direct first hand experience, not by proxy through the mother as a mediator of that world. These children learn skills, are given responsibilities and could never be regarded as hindrances to the smooth running of the community. Five, six and seven year old children in peasant communities make productive and useful contributions. In Southern Italy, Greece, Africa, South America, China and many other places, small children are often in complete charge of domestic animals (goats, sheep and so on). In the West Indies and elsewhere, girls of six and seven take full care of their younger siblings while their parents are occupied in the fields. And as soon as they are able to carry small loads, children work alongside the adults in addition to attending school. (In the West Indies, particularly, school attendance is erratic because children have always contributed to the agricultural work.)

But when a young child in this society attempts an 'adult' activity, he or she is either actively discouraged or tolerated with detached amusement. That we should *laugh* at our children for doing what children everywhere else in the world do as a matter of course is a symptom of our deep distrust of them. And we view with horror the idea that children should be given major responsibilities – their 'innocence' (i.e. separateness) has to be protected. We regard the integration of children into the larger society – the idea that children might *work* – as cruelty and yet view our own cruelty to them, our refusal to treat them honestly, our compulsion to buy them off with toys and promises, our belief in hiving them off away from the adult world in the home and in school as 'love'.

But we do not have to look as far as peasant societies in distant countries to learn about the capacities of small children. In Britain and the rest of Europe in the Middle Ages, as we saw earlier, the whole concept of childhood was largely meaningless. It was regarded as an apprenticeship for adulthood, a time of learning how to be of service to the community. But the example and experience of one family (large though it was), was not thought sufficient and, at the age of six or seven, children were boarded out with other families so that they might learn how to be of service to others. This practice continued, in a diluted form and for different reasons, right up to the 20th century. There are many records of working class families boarding their children out with relatives and friends while the propertied classes continued the long standing tradition of sending children away at the age of seven to learn 'manners, leadership and discipline'. But in place of the large family unit, made up of everything from a blacksmith to a cook, all engaged in productive work necessary for survival, there arose the educational institution – that is, an institution, set apart from adult society, dedicated to the task of moulding children (boys) for an imperialist economy. At the same time, there were poor children in the large cities who literally "brought themselves up", children of seven or so who lived by their wits on the streets without the benefit of parental guidance and protection.

Thea Thompson, writing on the 'Lost World of Childhood' in *New Society*, noted:

❝In respectable families, where poverty was due to unemployment, the parents as well as the children might depend on a child's wage. From the age of nine, an Essex farmworker's son worked 30 hours a week as a kitchen boy for two shillings a week. His brother had a job helping a baker. This brought in half a crown. For many weeks of the winter their earnings, the only money coming into the household, bought all the meat and bread for a family of six people.

Many other social and regional variations in the relationships between parents and children are revealed by our archive of notes and tape recordings. There are also aspects of great significance for which there is no space to discuss here. But one final dimension must be mentioned, if only because of the contrast with present day assumptions. The dependence of the child on its mother and father for emotional growth and stability was not consciously acknowledged by most parents before 1918.❞[1]

And it is only since that date that the capacities of children have been progressively underestimated and distorted by the emphasis on the child's dependence on its mother. I am not suggesting, as Thea Thompson's quote might imply, that children should go out to work full time, but merely that by subjecting modern children to a regime of uninterrupted control (inferiority), they have, in fact, lost touch with a great deal of their potential.

With regard to children's capacity to do much more for themselves than we either give them credit for or allow them, Thea Thompson also notes:

‘The children of the poor, however, were very much less dependent on their parents, and for a far shorter period. For moral and social training, they depended less on their parents than on children of the same age; and for food they depended on missions where free suppers were to be had, on soup kitchens, on school meals, on restaurant kitchens where food was sometimes given away, and on what they could scrounge and steal. The police would sometimes supply clothing and boots, and in large cities there were many ways of earning money.

Mr. Williams' childhood was typical of many in the extreme independent-separated category. The son of a coal heaver, he describes his parents as the "two biggest drunkards in the borough". He was the youngest of 13 children who had all dispersed by the time they were twelve – some to truant schools, others to homes of older brothers and sisters. Mr. Williams had an ingenious method of simulating ringworm on his skin which deceived school authorities: "I was away from school three or four months at a time. Yes. Over Covent Garden with a sack, a sackful of broken up wood, you know, flowerboxes, back over Waterloo Bridge, down Tenison Street, where Waterloo Station is now, knock at a door, 'Firewood ma'am?' 'How much?' 'Twopence the bagful'. 'No, give you a penny and three half pence'. 'No'. 'All right'. Shoot it down the area and back over the Garden four or five times and earn about eight pence or something like that . . . that's how we used to get hold of money. No, we never used to get anything out of our parents. Not pocket money anyway. They never had enough for their beer."

As a boy, Mr. Williams also sold newspapers and hired a barrow to sell hearthstone and vinegar. He supported himself – "fetched himself up" as he put it. 9

Mr. Williams, as Thompson notes, was typical of many thousands of children who responded to the awful conditions at the beginning of the century with an ingenuity, resourcefulness and independence unimaginable in children today. We turn our backs on the history of childhood at some great cost. All we can do is point to our child-centred theories as evidence of a new compassion for children. But just what is it our children have actually gained? How is it that a child of six or so could do most things for itself fifty or so years ago and relied on his nine and ten-year-old brothers and sisters for the things he could not do? And how is it that children in other societies take on responsible and vital work for the community while our children come to school at five unable to dress themselves properly, feed themselves adequately, co-operate in joint activity and are often quite incapable of carrying even small responsibilities?

As an infant teacher, I speak from direct experience. Even small jobs like watering the plants, returning used equipment to the cupboards, mixing paint and glue are light years beyond the capacity of today's five-year old, regardless of the child's class background.

Denied first hand experience of the outside world, the urban child battens on to the mother as the only source of information about the world, tormenting her with apparently trivial demands for attention: "I don't want these socks", "Can I have a lolly?" "Why is it raining?" The child, at the mercy of one person's arbitrary authority, turns awkward. It rejects the carefully prepared food in preference for ice cream and sweets, demands the latest, most fashionable toy and practises on the mother what it has seen the mother practising on the husband – emotional blackmail. It is a dynamic of mutual tyranny, with bribery and blackmail as the central themes. The mother resorts to bribing the child with promises of this or that if . . . and the child blackmails the mother in defiance of her superior position. Children learn very quickly which are their mothers' sensitive spots and then exploit them mercilessly. Thus, when the mother's attention is on other things, the child can instantly turn the situation to his advantage by whining, grisling, attempting a forbidden activity (playing with breakables, valuable objects, genitals or matches) or whatever most affects the mother. If all the child gets is a brusque telling-off, at least it was some *attention*, something to brighten an otherwise oppressively dull and boring day.

A child psychologist noted on the radio (during a discussion about nursery schools) that the language development of pre-school children was "woefully lacking" and he commented that "today's young mothers simply do not *talk* to their children". To this, I can add that children come to school at five not knowing their surnames, their addresses, or what town they live in and are incapable of sustaining even simple conversations or remembering easy instructions. And this has little to do with what educationalists call 'intelligence'.

Child psychologists, and many teachers, not seeing the wood for the trees, regurgitate established dogma and blame these children's deficiencies on their mothers. Do they imagine that all mothers are fully versed in their formulations of child psychology, that women have unlimited time and that they are not burdened with other children, financial and psychological dependence and that they have nothing more urgent to do than play and talk all day with their children? But society's expectations of good motherhood, besides being contradictory, are also totally *unrealistic*. No woman at home on her own can possibly hope to provide a sufficiently stimulating environment to compensate for the child's exclusion from the outside world. And no woman who is herself, by virtue of her isolation, denied the opportunity to talk and exchange ideas with her equals, can hope to talk constructively with her children. What experience have they to share with each other except their joint oppression? Caring single-handedly for children in this society deprives women of their own adulthood. Because the fact of being a mother relegates her to her own kind of pseudo childhood – like her children, she is denied day time access to adult centres, libraries, public meetings, restaurants, pubs, adult education classes and cinemas (except for children's shows!). She is deprived of an independent income and, like her children, is condemned solely to the company of others in the same situation.

Children, not surprisingly, emerge at five years of age from this prison "woefully lacking" in language development, possessive, aggressive, ignorant of the world around them and other people's needs, frequently unco-operative, babyishly dependent and ego-centric. Almost all young children in our society, by virtue of their upbringing, share these qualities to some extent. And so we deem these qualities normal. Thus our method of dealing with the outcome of our child rearing practices is to label these characteristics as natural. We have come, by a strange and devious route, to believe that

that is the way children *are*. And for those in doubt, there is a whole literature of child development and child psychology which supports this idea of 'normality'. Gesell, Piaget, Bowlby, Spock and many others (whose books are taken as gospel by students of child education and psychology in the Universities and Colleges of Education) have all worked on child development, having studied children who are growing up under conditions they lay down as desirable, and these writers have given us the standard dogma of the 'natural' condition of childhood.

Out of this comes a very important text, 'The Developmental Progress of Infants and Young Children', which is the standard guide for all professional workers in child care – paediatricians, Child Care Officers, child guidance specialists and workers in baby clinics. The booklet is described by its author, Dr. Mary Sheridan, as a 'paediatric tool' by which medical and social workers can easily detect early childhood abnormalities. The document, in tabulated form, lists every stage of development from birth to five years and gives us a precise picture of what childhood has come to mean. And, because of its authoritative stance, the tacit implication is that the norms it sets out for childhood would hold good in other cultures, and are therefore universal. There is no suggestion that the unattractive manifestations it lists may be brought about not by the natural development of the child's capacities, but by the peculiar conditions under which it is reared.

These are some of the aspects of social behaviour which the guide lists as normal:

at 9 months   "Clearly distinguishes strangers from familiars and requires reassurance before accepting their advances. Clings to known adult and hides face."

at 15 months   "Closely dependent on adult's reassuring presence. . . . Needs constant supervision to protect child from dangers of extended exploration and exploitation of environment."

at 18 months   "Emotionally still very dependent on familiar adult, especially Mother."

at 2 years   "Constantly demanding Mother's attention. Defends own possessions with determination. As yet no idea of sharing. Plays near other children but not with them. Resentful of attention shown to other children."

at 2½ years   "Throws violent tantrums when thwarted or unable to express urgent needs and less easily distracted.
"Watches other children at play interestedly and occasionally joins in for a few minutes, but little notion of sharing playthings or adult's attention."

at 4 years   "Needs other children to play with and is alternately co-operative and aggressive with them as with adults."

I would submit that not one of these manifestations in social behaviour is the normal condition of childhood. (Indeed, as an example of desirable upbringing, such a child would be regarded as severely disturbed by many peoples of the world.)

The nine-month-old baby is only fearful of strangers because her world is so limited. She will cling to the known adult because she only knows one adult! The 15-month-old baby is similarly dependent on one adult's reassuring presence because there's only one adult around. If her world were larger, with older brothers and sisters and friends and neighbours to whom she could turn, then there would be no question of her leech-like adherence to one person. That a two year old child will only play near other children and has no idea of sharing is nonsense. Mary Sheridan assumes that what children are *prevented* from doing – that is, playing and relating with children and adults of all ages – they are *unable* to do.

Many two year old children who come from large families or who live communally with other families or attend day nurseries have been playing *with* other children, and sharing things with them since they were one year old. They are not advanced, but merely privileged to share the company of many other people – adults and children – in a world which elsewhere deliberately under-privileges children, depriving them of varied human company. At $2\frac{1}{2}$ years old we see that the child is throwing "violent tantrums", has "little notion of sharing" and, at 4 years is "alternately co-operative and aggressive". What a picture. Indeed, the child is merely an early version of society's most highly prized adult – aggressive, possessive, competitive, individualistic and materialistic, with an underside of co-operativeness which only emerges in the privacy of the family, between sorties into the outside world. Now these are, very obviously, *acquired and learned* characteristics. They have nothing to do with the child's basic nature but everything to do with the conditions under which the child is reared and the society he is being prepared for.

For those children who are fortunate enough not to be subjected to five years of enforced isolation and privatization with their mothers, the norms of child development laid down by the experts would be both inappropriate and incomprehensible. Because such children are spared the resentful (or even loving) attention of *one* authoritative person, because they have grown up with several people of all ages to whom they could turn for attention, guidance and learning, because concepts of private property are alien to them (as in China, communes, the kibbutz and many pre-literate cultures), because displays of aggression are quite out of place in societies which are founded on mutual co-operation and not self-interest, these children progress through childhood incapable of a tantrum, a selfish act or the emotional blackmail which characterise childhood in Western society. In communities which do not divide young children from each other as well as from adults we will not see children "resentful of attention shown to other children", and where they are not denied access to meaningful activity we will not see "violent tantrums".

Children, spared our upbringing, will also be capable of trust, self-reliance, and independence undreamed of in our society. (Visitors to modern China returned amazed at the skill and competence of even very young children there who, *unsupervised*, travel about the towns and villages, going from nursery and school to fields and home.) They will have no interest in resorting to manipulative behaviour, tormenting adults with impossible demands. And they will not be woefully lacking in language development because people will have talked with them instead of shouting at them to keep their inferior place.

Now I do not want to give the impression that all

children in our society are 'bad' and that all children in other societies are 'good'. It is thankfully true that many of our children survive without being unduly distorted by their upbringing. Their capacity to co-operate with others, their generosity and uncompetitive interest in others, their pleasure in sharing things, their curiosity and unextinguished joy in play and conversation emerge unscathed, but my point is that these qualities remain in spite of the counteractive pressures they are subjected to. They owe little or nothing to the dogma of child psychology or the emphasis in schools on an exclusively competitive approach to life and learning. They owe everything to the resilience of the child, the family, the commune and the nursery, to hang on to some basic, and I submit, 'natural' humanitarian values and to resist the multiplicity of pressures which seek to tear those values down.

* * * * * * *

The Family

Ideology of the Family

THE family, as the cornerstone of society and its fundamental social unit, provides an unending source of research, a subject for radical psychiatry and the chief target for commercial bombardment. And we are all born into a family and are either in another one, or in transit between or, having outlived the cycle, are waiting to join the big one in the sky.

Because the family is deemed the *only* organisation in which to live, all those who live outside it are either odd, abnormal or, in the worst cases, social outcasts. Our self-image depends, to a large extent, on where we are in the family cycle – daughter/wife/mother/widow. The young who are growing out of their first family and are plainly on their way to their second, that of their own making, are the only large body of people whose existence outside the family structure is countenanced. But we have categories for the rest – those who, whether or not they chose to, find they have missed the boat – spinsters, divorced people, single women with children, lesbians and homosexuals, childless couples, middle aged bachelors and ageing widows and widowers. Whatever their personal circumstances, these people are daily reminded, with everything from ideal happy family type advertisements to banter from their workmates, that they don't fit into society's straitjacket. ("Waiting for Mr. Right, are you?", "We'd prefer a family man for this job," "This one'll get you to the altar. You can't hold out much longer!") They are the curiosities and casualties of a family centred society.

The fate of the widowed is sealed with condescension and pity. But they are largely ignored, first because they are an inconvenient reminder of what lies in store for everyone else, but mainly because they occupy their place outside the family structure only reluctantly and certainly blamelessly. But for the rest of these people – homosexuals, lesbians, unsupported mothers and so on, society reserves a battery of neglect, suspicion and derision, all of which stems from a basic distrust. It doesn't matter whether they have refused to conform to the ideal or whether they are unable to. The conclusion which is imposed on them and with which they have to live, is that they have *failed* to. Single and divorced people are supposed to be lonely and bitter and if they're not, then there must be something wrong with them. Homosexuals and lesbians' only usefulness is as a subject for dirty jokes and voyeuristic gossip. Not only are they outside the family, but because they threaten it, they were until recently, outside the *law*. (Changes in the law have done little to change attitudes.) Childless couples, too, are pitied or badgered with questions and suffer endless innuendoes about 'the patter of tiny feet'. The power of the ideal takes many forms. Whether it is a 'tut-tut' and the shaking of heads, or the nod and the wink, or whispered condolences, only those who have achieved the blessed state of the complete family are immune. One-child families are always considered incomplete. ("Don't you think it's cruel/selfish/niggardly to have an 'only' child?") To have to defend one's 'deviant' life style, in the face of society's opposition, is a profound imposition. The supposed freedom of the individual to arrange his or her life according to personal inclination is a pernicious myth, compounded by the absence of choice. For the freedom of the individual is merely the freedom to pursue one ideal – private house, spouse and two or three children.

It is because the family is the only sanctioned unit for living that everything which threatens it takes the proportions of a serious social problem. Judging from the publicity accorded to them, and the way in which people get steamed up, the issues of the day are not poverty, racial and sexual discrimination, and imperialism, but illegitimacy, abortion, permissiveness, homosexuality, pornography, promiscuity and drugs, all of which must be stamped out, cured, labelled obscene or made illegal. Even contraception and divorce, despite the paraded permissive society, make people lower their voices; contraception, because if it were free and readily available, would undermine women's dependence on men, giving rise to the spectre of every historical age – the 'free' woman, and divorce because it is an index of family breakdown, i.e. failure. Despite legal reforms, illegitimacy and divorce are always considered regrettable. And just why are unmarried mothers considered such a serious problem? And why should children born out of wedlock have to hide the fact? And why do non-heterosexual people have to resort to furtive secrecy? And why are promiscuity and broken homes dirty words? And why shouldn't women have complete control of their bodies? The thread which connects all these things is that each one poses a threat which, if allowed free reign and social acceptability, would seriously erode the inflexibility of family life.

At the heart of so much conservative cant – displayed in the grandeur of the self-appointed guardians of our moral welfare – is a real fear for the stability of the family. And there are good reasons for their fear. Their belief that anything which threatens the family also threatens society is well founded. For the family, as its defenders tell us, is the backbone of society. To shake the family, question it, attack it and analyse it is to show that personal relationships and the generation game do not take place in a vacuum. When we expose the rot and decay in the family and its functions, we reveal the rot and decay which form the foundations on which our society is built. Thus divorce, illegitimacy and homosexuality are not testaments to individual freedom but protagonists of doom.

* * * * * * *

The propaganda which is woven around the family draws a cosy veil of timelessness over hearth, kitchen and nursery, a self-enclosing world of privacy, insulated from the intrusions of the outside world. With only TV bulletins (which de-signify war, disaster and rebellion) to penetrate its defences against the world, the home and family is, at one and the same time, a safe harbour and a fortress. Sociologists can contemplate its complexities (writing papers with titles like *Role Theory and Patterns of Conjugal Role Relationships*), psychiatrists can call it 'a lethal gas chamber', but the idealised image remains intact, an image which every advertiser wears closest to his heart – mother in her twenties, upstanding father in his early thirties and two children, inevitably a bright boy and a sweet girl. But we are not just talking about the advertising image. We are talking about what the family *means*, what, in fact, it symbolises for everyone. Almost without variation it consists of two generations living in harmony in a home they own, with an assortment of mechanical aids to comfortable living. It's an image which wears astonishingly well, considering its unreality and that less than 10% of the population have, or will ever achieve, such a life style.

Children who come from overcrowded back-to-back terrace houses in depressed, industrial towns share the same picture image of the family as do their middle class counterparts, who live in small flats in large cities. I have a large collection of drawings of families and houses from primary school children in three very different areas (London, Leeds and the rural South West). The image these drawings present is substantially the same as the one we see flashed on our screens, in story books and the same as the one which we have all carried in our heads as long as we can remember – detached house, handsome, well dressed father – aproned, smiling mother – a boy of about 8 and a girl of about 6 – a gleaming car in the garage and the whole lot surrounded by a neat white fence with tulips in the garden and a bright sun overhead. No old people, no cross words, no rain, no illness, no poverty and no-one ever grows any older – a static dream to cherish which is never quite fantasy because it's always around the corner or somebody else has it.

How badly are we fooled by the dream? And why is it so important that we should be? The answers to these questions, as this chapter will attempt to show, hinge on the fact that, in a capitalist society, the family fulfils an economic function. The family owes its existence to an economic system which needs the family to muffle the discontents of the work force, to train the young to take their allotted place, to feed, service and prepare the present and future labour force, to consume large quantities of material goods, to transmit the social order and values (possessiveness, competitiveness, private property, etc.) to the young, to keep people in line sexually and to restrict women's aspirations. And so our eyes are blinkered in order to keep them riveted on the ideal, an ideal which, despite our own lives and the living evidence around us, remains untarnished by the reality.

The economics of the family are hidden behind its

psychological and emotional attractions; it beckons us and beguiles us with its promise of private happiness and personal fulfilment. Knowing that, we are taught to believe that the small family unit – parents living with their dependent children – is the only normal pattern for living and one that is practised by the majority of the population. But it isn't so. The startling fact is that less than one quarter of the country's households have dependent children.

⁶In fact, over half of all dependent children are in less than 13% of all households. Rather a small minority of adults are at any one time carrying most of the responsibility for rearing the next generation.

The propagation of the population is also heavily dependent in Western Countries on a rather small minority of adults who chose to have three or more children. These families have to compensate for the very large number of adults, indeed about half the persons of recent generations, who do not reproduce themselves. There are large numbers of persons who never marry, or marry and have no children, and a similar number of couples who have only one child. ... At any one time less than 9% of all households in the United Kingdom include three or more children dependent on them; these households are bringing up over 40% of the next generation.⁹[1]

All of which raises some very interesting questions. (Judging from these facts, more people have missed the boat than are in it.) We should ask why we are taught to model ourselves, our lives and our aspirations on something which, at any one time, is practised by a minority of the population. Why this minority and not, say, the minority who share flats and houses or those who live in large groups or those who live alone? A great deal of television, both advertising and programme material, is aimed at the 'average family audience', the implicit assumption being that they are in the majority. In addition, about seventy per cent of television adverts are directed at the young family and more directly, at the housewife at home with young children. After a week's viewing, no-one could be blamed for honestly thinking that three quarters of all women were housebound mothers. Why don't adverts and programmes focus exclusively on other minorities? Old people? Single men and women? Couples whose children have grown up and left home? Significantly, not only is this propaganda aimed at a very small section of the society, but it is also aimed at the *poorest*.

> **'**At any one time most adults have no parental responsibilities. Most earned and unearned incomes are received by adults with no children to support. Most of the nation's wealth flows to non-parents.**'**[2]

Those with the greatest spending power are, by definition, those without children to support. The two 'richest' periods in an adult's life are before marriage but, chiefly, the period after children have left home, before the final pensioned poverty. And the poorest period, significantly, is the one where financial and emotional insecurity is at its most rampant, when material needs are most keenly felt and when adults are most accessible to commercial propaganda and most vulnerable to exploitation.

The family follows its own remorseless cycle – birth, growth, change, breakdown and death, with clear demarcation lines between its stages. After childhood spent in one's first family and after a brief period of independence, we get together with someone in similar circumstances to form a second family. Its life span is probably only about twenty years. When the children are grown there are twenty or thirty years remaining where the family is something which exists only at Christmas. And when one of the partners dies, the cycle is all but over.

In one individual life span of seventy years, perhaps only half of those years have been spent in an intact family unit. The period when the (second) family is together is the shortest period in the whole cycle, but it is the one by which the rest is measured. If we see the whole cycle as a film with a beginning, middle and an end, then we can see that the time when parents and dependent children are living together has been caught in a static frame and blown up out of all proportion, and is so projected as to designify the rest of the film. So it is that the family unit is the peak of the pyramid of the social hierarchy against which individual lives appear as one long 'before and after'.

* * * * * * *

We can look at the institution of the small nuclear family in two ways – first, how it looks from the outside, what functions it performs, why it is so essential to the system under which we live and second, how it looks from the inside – that is, how the individual woman, child or man experiences it. And we can see how the single interconnecting knot which binds the family to society is tied, at society's end, with economics and is understood, at the family's end, as emotion.

On the face of it, the organisation of people on a mass scale into small, privatized and apparently autonomous units, appears natural, inevitable, convenient and

214

desirable. Each individual probably feels that he or she 'fell into' the family structures, as much by accident as by choice, as though the events which determine a person's life take on a reality which is independent of the person's wishing. We are all, it seems, sucked along by an immense tidal wave which prevents us even from conceiving of a different life style. Because we can't remember being forced to marry, have children and so on, we think we must have chosen to. Families, apparently, happen to people. You 'fall in love', children 'come along'. One chooses to live within the family structure because one would otherwise have to choose *not* to fall in love, *not* to buy a house, *not* to have children and so on. It is not the freedom to choose between different varieties of cake but the freedom to have a piece of cake or no cake at all. What it means is that we do not 'fall into' the family. We are taken by the hand and firmly led into it. And when we are so entangled in its ideology that all our attitudes and personal relationships are shaped by it, it's hard to see that the family group may be just one of many possible alternatives for social living. But it is precisely because the small family performs essential functions for society which other social groupings would not do, that it is so fundamental to our view of ourselves and the world.

To the question 'What are families for?' many people would sincerely answer 'For love and for rearing children', and there the subject would end. So I am deeply conscious that descriptions of the additional functions that the family performs may be as repugnant as defining sex as a mechanical act for producing babies. But to accept the idealised image of the family as just a vehicle for the expression of love is, firstly, to deny our own experience and, secondly, to surrender willingly to mystification; a mystification which breeds on a whole nexus of assumptions, first woven within the privacy of the family itself and reinforced by the outside world, that is, that the family exists in a *vacuum* for itself, that the relations between individual members of the family are wholly determined by their personalities and who they are, rather than by theirs and the whole family's relationship to the outside world. These assumptions lay the basis for our understanding of ourselves and form the outer covering of our protection, as though all families were neatly contained in an autonomous and free floating bubble, within which the members of the family are free to bicker or love each other according to their private inclinations and whose links with other bubbles are merely contractual. Two bubbles may temporarily touch each other, grow larger through marriage and then separate, eventually to drift down in age and poverty to vanish on the scrap heap below. But the bubble is neither free nor self-contained. Each bubble is firmly connected to every other and, with arms linked, sacrificially dances attendance on the system which calls the tune.

But everything conspires to teach us otherwise. If we want to understand who we are, how our personalities are shaped, we are taught to look back to our families and trace our character development through the influences of our parents, brothers and sisters, with only a sidelong glance at school, teachers, peer group, media pressures and so on. If we are aggressive it is because our parents didn't love us enough. If we are timid it is because our parents didn't love us enough. If we are sexually repressed and inhibited it is because our parents made us feel guilty, and so on, *ad nauseam*. So-called radical psychiatrists perpetuate the bubble-like view of the family by attributing schizophrenia to the idiosyncracies and short comings of the 'patient's' family relationships. Whatever the case, the illusion remains intact.

Each family is unique and each family is different from every other family. Within the terms of the illusion, we can attribute all personal hangups to our home background – in fact, to the *differences* between families and not to the similarities. But it is wrong to attribute our private inhibitions or our 'inadequacies' to parental influences. Most people's 'personal problems' stem from being forced into constricting roles which, though enacted within the family, are but symptoms of the diseased state of society.

For instance, almost everyone in this society has had their sexuality distorted. When sex (usually symbolised by a woman's thighs or breasts) is a commodity to be bought, manipulated for commercial ends, and sold with everything from cars to deodorants and when it is the most common subject for jokes, when words like 'poke', 'grind' and 'screw' are commonplace, then parents who stop their children from masturbating or exploring each other's genitals, are merely dancing to the system's tune. It is not our families who are responsible for distorting our sexuality, but a sexually corrupted society.

But yes, we are shaped by our families, but families are shaped by the system. The opposite way of looking at the same phenomena is to open the bubble and see that each one, though separate, is a variation on a theme, and a grotesque one at that. It is profoundly disturbing to discover that the outer shell of one family is substantially the same for all families, that the public thread which connects them all determines much of the private experience; most disturbing of all, not only do the similarities between families outweigh the differences but the similarities correspond precisely to the common functions which all families perform.

The desultory nod to the family as a microcosm of society and the piercing eye on the peculiarities of each one merely serves to perpetuate the comfortable bubble-like image. I want turn the whole thing over and take the microscope to the microcosm and, in redressing the balance, bypass for the moment, differences between families. Perhaps, anyway, the differences are merely the spots and blemishes which distinguish one bubble from another.

* * * * * * *

Monogamy

THE strongest strand in the connecting thread is monogamy – one man and one woman loving each other in an intensively exclusive way, and if not, then at least living together. We have no choice but to believe in monogamy, even when we don't or can't practise it. Within the confines of the monogamous principle, it is surprising how many contradictions can be tolerated but how little they affect the principle. We may, by chance, discover that there is nothing exclusive about sex, that sexual relations only breed jealousy when love means private property, that it is possible to love more than one person at a time and that affection need not be dependent on measuring its return.

Under pressure, the monogamous principle has had to bend a little. Where once marriage was 'for life', an endurance test called 'for better or worse', we can now change partners on condition that we do not do it too often and that we continue to pay lip service to the principle by having only one partner at a time. The ultimate justification for the one woman/one man principle is that love is quantifiable, something which each person can weigh and give out but only if it is returned. In fact, monogamy has come to be the definition of love, a yardstick by which we measure the rest of our emotions. 'Real' love is only that which is exclusively focused on one person of the opposite sex – all else is labelled 'liking'. Like so much butter, romantic love must be spread thickly on one slice of bread; to spread it over several is to spread it 'thinly'. But experience is always at odds with the principle. In rare moments, when the external categories which fragment our emotions fall away, we do glimpse the possibilities of whole feelings. A man loves God but does he love his wife less because of it? A woman loves her children. Must she love their father less? Is the tenderness I feel towards a friend's suffering of a different order than the tenderness I feel for my lover? Are the well springs of grief released only for the death of loved ones or what is it about the bombing of villages which makes me cry? We are divided from ourselves and from each other by the fragmentation of our emotions – the external categories by which we define ourselves and which dam up our feelings so effectively that only in extremis are our emotions allowed to overflow.

Romantic, monogamous love is an imposed law – the means by which we are allowed to recompose the fragmentation of our selves into an apparent whole. So that jealousy comes to be regarded as the objective proof of love instead of an excrescence on our emotions. So that sex is legitimized, so that attraction and warmth and affection can be called 'love', which can then be parcelled into marriage and one woman and one man come to symbolise an *institution*.

‘Lumbered by convention and my misery, we blundered into a relationship with all the accretions of permanence: meetings with families, and holidays together; the barnacles attach themselves to the hull and the ship slows down and crawls to a halt.’[1]

The origins of the ideal of romantic love have been well documented. That love and marriage were once anathema to each other, that love could only flourish when it departed from convention is well known. Marriage was a contractual arrangement, largely confined to the propertied classes, and was based on suitability and financial considerations. The partners were expected to respect each other and, hopefully, be compatible. It is not my purpose here to trace the history of romantic love but merely to re-state a commonplace. Where once marriage for love was the exception, it is now the rule. In theory, at least, for we are not out of the wood yet. On one level we pity women from other cultures who, despite their education in this country, must still submit to arranged marriages to men they may never have met. On another level, the romantic imagination is still caught by the flowering of unpermitted love, love which flouts convention and is tinged with tragedy. The heiress and the bus driver, the King and the divorcee, the intellectual and the sex symbol. The ideal of love, home, marriage and children may persist but where does that leave passion? For we haven't, in joining love with marriage, succeeded in eliminating passion. Because it cannot co-exist with the ideal it is either ruled out or vicariously experienced through plays, films, novels or private fantasy. Why else is the unhappy marriage or the doomed relationship of more interest than the happy, love-matched marriage?

But the ideal is effortlessly pervasive. And to aspire to it requires a frantic search for a love object, someone who will be a repository for the realisation of our whole selves. The reward can never quite match up to the expectations, but to admit it is to admit that we are all fooled. So we sublimate our passion by fierce concentration on the partner. If it isn't the perfect relationship then either we invest all our energies in trying to transform it or we dwell on its inadequacies. Either way, the gates of the trap have closed. Monogamy triumphs, even in failure.

Perhaps not everyone is completely taken in by the ideal. For there is a tacit acceptance that romantic love can perish within the confines of mortgages and domesticity, and that to tie it down is to squeeze the spirit out of it. Adolescents look at their parents, neighbours and family friends and lament the dearth of happy marriages, swearing either that they will never marry or that they will wait until they really do find Mr. or Mrs. Right. They're going to make dead sure that they don't end up like their parents. By the time they're in their twenties, their ideals may have taken a battering. Apparently, the only alternative is loneliness, or promiscuity, social exclusion and insecurity, all of which closes in on them so fast that marriage appears the only sensible solution, even if Mr. Right was a little wrong. And the plans for a life of 'adventure and excitement' disintegrate into night-time fantasies, luring their victims to sleep and eventual oblivion. The image of the man or woman who has sacrificed an exciting life as an actress or explorer for marriage and its attendant responsibilities, and who finishes up embittered, is a classic cliche but no less true for that. We must, after all, resign ourselves to the inevitable and compromise our private selves with our public personae and, to save embarrassment all round, maintain that we are merely 'settling down' before it's too late. And if we do end up like our parents, then that's the price of freedom. Or so the story goes.

Is it really as bleak as that? Is monogamy inevitably destructive? Given real *choices* I believe it need not be but under the weight of social pressure and expectation, it almost always is. Because monogamy, which leads to responsible marriage, is a fundamental form of *social control*. To be sure, there are many couples who have managed to salvage the best from the situation they have been pressured into. The lifelong union of a man and a woman may well result in a happiness which touches all those with whom they have contact. But it is rare and it is always a testament to their resilience. If we were not conditioned into the monogamous principle, if many more expressions of love and affection were permissible in a more fluid atmosphere of what is, and is not, acceptable (for instance, open relationships between people of the same sex, or with more than one person at a time), then monogamy, instead of being a safety net for loneliness, would merely be one of many alternatives which people might well choose *freely*.

In the absence of real choice, monogamous love is institutionalised. We believe that we have come a long way since the time of loveless, arranged marriage, but many sociological studies of 'mate selection' show very clearly that romantic love and marriage co-exist as uneasily as they ever did. 'Falling in love', blind attraction and love-conquers-all are not the stuff of marriage at all. It turns out that we find 'the only one' by a strict but unconscious process of elimination until we end up with someone from a similar social and educational background, age, colour, race and even religion, a process which, given the limitations on social contact, narrows the field down to maybe a maximum of two or three partners. Optimistically, love is the last additional factor and the only one which differentiates modern marriage from earlier versions. Marriage between people of vastly different age, class, race or education is frowned on. Though the woman may swear 'But we *love* each other!', it's not enough to heal the rift, for society's approval depends now, just as it did in the Victorian era, on the *suitability* of the partners. Only when the fundamental criteria of suitability are satisfied is love admissible. And on those terms love is expressed as 'enjoying being together' and 'liking the same things'.[2] Hardly the blinding revelation that the myth of 'falling in love' suggests. We have not travelled so far from the Victorian era as we would like to think, for the fundamentals of marriage have barely changed. We have, instead, new labels on an old product.

Dissatisfactions with marriage are acceptable because they are predictable. The fortyish man who lusts after young girls, the frustrated housewife who yearns to be courted again, are comic figures in the landscape; their temptations are crudely rewarded by a profitable industry of girlie magazines, striptease clubs, romantic novels and singing idols (Tom Jones, Andy Williams etc.). Instead of being encouraged to question the monogamous principle, we are given fantasy outlets for the frustrations it imposes. And as long as people do not question the principle, they will continue to feel guilty or personally inadequate when they discover that marriage is not the complete answer to their sexual needs and that married love is not the all-embracing light at the end of their private tunnel.

We may lie awake at night wondering where we went wrong, why it hasn't worked out as well as it *ought* to have done and, in desperation, list our partner's good and bad qualities and weigh them up; or we may nostalgically remember the loving, carefree days and resolve to resuscitate the affection that has so long been submerged by the daily grind, feeling guilty because we've been blaming the other instead of ourselves, knowing that perhaps it is a bit of each but never, never questioning why it ought to work and why two people *have* to make the best of living together. We don't see that the expectations – the baggage that we all bring to marriage – are impossible to live up to. If we didn't expect to find personal salvation through married love we wouldn't be disappointed in not finding it.

But marriage itself must remain above suspicion.

Sociologists can busy themselves looking at the incidence of divorce and family breakdown and write studies on the far more widespread phenomena of 'marital dissatisfaction' among couples who nevertheless remain married, but the main question remains unasked. Is it marriage that is wrong and not the people in it?

Monogamy is the life force of the family and people stay married because marriage is, everywhere, the most universal and most effective means of social control. Underneath the myths, fantasies and formulas by which we live our lives lurk the real facts. The State has the first claim on marriage for it is the only effective method known for compelling people to perform the 'functions required of them in society'. *It makes women into wives and mothers and men into breadwinners.*

Admissions that marriage is a form of social control are hard to come by, but John Eekelaar, writing a solid book on family law for the Penguin Education series, let one slip:

❝The family is a social organism which arises to fulfil certain needs of society and of individuals and which is subject to natural processes of decay and ultimate dissolution. Society cannot eradicate these processes, yet it can, by *social pressure and by law*, so channel them as to lessen the risk of family disruption. To this end it employs the purely legal concept of marriage to confer special recognition upon certain family groups *in order to enable them better to perform some of the functions required of them in society.*❞ (my emphasis.)

Marriage is the first and basic model of the division of labour and power between the sexes, the legalised sanction whereby society justifies the public separation of men from women by throwing them together in private. Within the institution of marriage, men and women are supposed to resolve the conflicts of the public domain, where the power, education and money are so massively weighted in favour of men – where men treat women as inferiors with impunity, giving orders to waitresses, secretaries, barmaids, cleaners and shop assistants alike, and where the commercial bombardment of nipples and thighs perpetuates the sexual gulf between men and women. Is a man who works on a building site, spending much of his day leering at women passers-by, to come home and treat his wife as an equal? Is a man who gives orders to women at work as habitually and as effortlessly as he pees, supposed to, as soon as he closes his front door, regard his wife as an equal? Is a woman who has deferred to her boss's judgment all day at work supposed not to defer to her husband's? Is a woman who has been conditioned to be a passive sexual object, receiving and occasionally deflecting men's attentions, suddenly supposed to take the sexual initiative when she is married? Is a woman who works all day in close contact with other women in the typing pool, the shop or factory, supposed to reserve her innermost thoughts for her husband whom she sees for only a few hours a day? Are we supposed to neglect the intimacy of the work place in order to concentrate on the home?

Without marriage as the private safety valve for public conflict, women would not tolerate the injustices of unequal pay, power and education and the degradation of sexual objectification – all the things in fact, which make up the sum total of their usefulness. Without marriage, human sexuality would not have to submit to social and physical restraint. Marriage is presented as society's panacea for these ills. Marriage does not solve these conflicts but the fact that it contains them, is what makes it such an effective and useful form of social control.

Any glance round society reveals that the sexes are placed on opposite poles with an enormous chasm of oppression, degradation and misunderstanding generated to keep them apart. Out of this, marriage plucks one woman and one man, ties them together with 'love' and asserts that they shall live in harmony and that they shall, for the rest of their lives, bridge that chasm with a mixture of betrayal, sex, affection, deceit and illusion. While marriage is supposed to heal the rift and while women, out of loyalty and affection, claim that it does indeed lead to harmony ("I'm writing to tell you I've got the most considerate husband in the world" – *Considerate?*), they are eager players in the game. Like the lone woman on a board of directors, marriage is society's tokenism. It's easy to rationalise the continued division of labour, power and money between men and women by pointing to marriage and suggesting that at *heart*, that is, in the private emotions which have no consequence on the outside world where the game is actually played, relations between men and women are just fine and dandy. From the sociologists' angle, the further apart men and women are in terms of work, education, personal goals and so on, the more popular is marriage. (People are marrying younger, living longer and most divorced people re-marry.) Because there is no real evidence for 'the battle of the sexes' it is assumed not to exist.

There is a battle but it takes place without spectators. Within marriage, it is women's duty to heal the rift between the sexes, to gloss over the differences with love and judgment and a few beguiling tactics. And because it is an impossible task and because failure in it reflects

227

badly on her, she struggles alone and unnoticed. In previous chapters we have seen several aspects of marriage, how women are victimised by the legal disadvantages and the unequal division of money. Perhaps the most basic struggle is over power, for it is here that marriage serves society most usefully. Magically, the power that is vested in men, in all spheres of life, is somehow supposed to be neutralised in marriage, thereby justifying its legitimacy outside the home.

As long as a man is seen to exert influence in his work and his social life, he can smile with the best of them and say that, at home, his wife wears the pants. It costs him nothing to defer to his wife's authority in the home because he has ample compensation outside it and, in any case, it keeps the little thing happy! And, in the total power game, the home is but a tiny part, which any generous and self-respecting man can relinquish. For the man at the bottom of the social ladder the situation is rather different. He is reduced to claiming authority merely on the basis of male authority, a situation which prevails and is condoned everywhere. The Newsomes and other researchers have found that the lower down the social scale, the more rigid are the attitudes towards women's domestic role – i.e. the claim for male superiority. These attitudes are less rigid amongst the professional classes but there is still a great discrepancy between what is preached and what is practised.

The power which men exert over women in marriage may be similar in kind, however it is obtained. Dair Gillespie wrote an article entitled 'Who Has the Power? The Marital Struggle' in which he re-examined data from studies of marriage. He found that the basic power struggle had been seriously neglected.

228

‘Professional men demand deference because of their work. This enables them to accept the doctrine of equality without having to live it.’[3]

As most women could have told him, this is the tune they all have to dance to, whether their husband is an assembly line worker or a business executive. The middle class man has the same access to power, which accrues to him *as a male*, as does his working class counterpart. But with great magnanimity he can turn to his wife and maintain that he isn't going to use it. And she is trapped for she can't complain about him dominating her like other men dominate their wives. She can only complain about the amount of time he spends on his work, his neglect of the children, their lack of communication, his boring business friends which she must entertain and the fact that he is always the centre of attention. But she can't say that he is consciously *dominating* her. To the outside world they would both genuinely maintain that theirs is a marriage of equals but, in areas of importance, she is as powerless as she ever was.

All women wage private struggles against male power. Mostly, they can only take the crumbs that men offer and if the battleground is over who is going to do the washing up or where they will go for their holidays (and such matters are usually the defining limit of female power), then that is where the struggle will take place. But it is always a partial struggle, for women can never wrest from men the right to determine where the battleground will be. That is always men's automatic privilege, the nucleus of their hidden power which they can call upon at will. Whether they resort to their maleness, physical strengths and threats or the demands of their work, the result is the same.

229

To their credit, some men have tried to equalise the stakes. They acknowledge the symptoms of the struggle, locating them at the kitchen sink, without ever seeing the disease itself. They see that their arguments for avoiding housework and child care are false and that their wife's work is probably harder and more arduous than their own (this is especially true of middle class men), so they have rolled up their sleeves and 'helped' in the house but in so doing they have invaded the woman's only sphere of influence. Gradually she sees her tiny corner of autonomy ebbing away. For by participating in the home, men bring to their activity their whole apparatus of male prerogative. He can't just get on with the work. He has to have a *say* in it as well. However eager he may be to help in the home, he is still notably reluctant to relinquish his economic and sexual advantage over women.

The man may try to dispense with his overt authority but he can hardly reject the power, so integral is it to the whole marital structure. As Dair Gillespie points out:

> ❝He is the economic head of the joint household and hence represents it in the view of society. She takes his name and belongs to his class. She follows him where his work calls to determine their place of residence. Their lives are geared to the daily, weekly, annual rhythms of his life.❞

Equality in marriage, the neutralisation of male power, is usually taken to mean that the partners share in decisions about their future, their home and their children. But the authority of the male does not hinge merely in decisions. A couple may decide on their children's education only once or twice in their married life. Similarly, if they decide to move house or change jobs or if they make three or four major joint decisions together, that is no index of equality. For sociologists (and consequently the prevailing ideology) have made the mistake of equating joint decision making with the death of the Victorian patriarchal family.

It is simply that the patriarchal model has taken a more subtle turn – has, in fact, gone underground. Dair Gillespie brings it out into the open in the conclusion to his article:

‘Thus it is clear that for a wife to gain even a modicum of power in the marital relationship, she must gain it from external sources, i.e. she must participate in the work force, her education must be superior to that of her husband, and her participation in organisations must excel his. Equality of resources leaves the power in the hands of the husband. The equalitarian marriage as a norm is a myth. Under some conditions individual women gain power *vis-a-vis* their husbands, but more power is not equal power. Equal power women do not have. Equal power women will not get so long as the present socioeconomic system remains.’

The struggle for ascendancy, the fruitless attempts to reconcile the differences, the silent hurts and the wells of resentment are the cracks in every marriage structure which love merely papers over. And when the paper wears thin to reveal the widening cracks, we have, we are told, no-one but ourselves to blame. Imprisoned in our bedrooms and kitchens, we attribute our discontents to the shortcomings of our partner, the bad influences of our mothers or our own private hangups which prevent us from coming to terms with marriage. Women will say that they can't communicate with their husbands and men will say that their wives 'don't understand them' and the same situation is played out over and over again in a million households where the story is the same and only the faces are different. The man will clench his teeth and kick the furniture and the woman will bite back her tears and when finally, at bed time, they make it up, the woman will tearfully admit that the children have made her edgy and tired and really it was just a petty quarrel and she promises not to let the 'little things' get her down again, and the man says he will try not to get so angry but he is so pushed at work and does need to relax at home, so if she could just be a little more welcoming when he comes home and not bother him too much with her little problems. . . . And so they fall asleep, in a fragile blanket of love which is stretched past breaking point and which will split open again in a week or a month to reveal another aching crack which they must again strain to close.

The bridge that marriage constructs across the chasm between the sexes is an illusion which most of us are constrained to enact as reality. By disguising the division between the sexes which this society perpetrates, it reinforces the apartheid of public life and removes the battleground to a 'safe' and insignificant place – the home; our private lives may be disrupted and in many cases, utterly destroyed by it, but all the while the wheels of the system will keep on turning smoothly. And as long as men and women row in private or submerge their differences in silence while putting on a married face to the outside world, the chasm between men and women will continue to serve the society that created it.

* * * * * * *

Economics of the Nuclear Family

WILLIAM Goode noted that throughout the world, industrialisation has heralded the breakdown of traditional family systems – everything from large, land tied, extended households to clan or tribal systems, all of which are giving way to the small mobile unit:

‘Family research in the post World War II period has documented one gross empirical regularity, whose processes are not yet clearly understood – that in all parts of the world and for the first time in world history all social systems are moving fast or slowly toward some form of the conjugal family system and also toward industrialisation.’

It is no accident. One of the first requirements of a capitalist economy is a mobile, docile workforce. Men and women who are 'free' to acquire the skills that the economy needs and who are prepared to move wherever their skills are most in demand. And this they cannot do if they are tied, either emotionally or by obligation, to the larger family network. Even in such a highly industrialised country as Britain, there are still many pockets of extended close knit families and communities, whose members are reluctant to uproot themselves. Significantly, they are in areas of depression and unemployment – Glasgow, South Wales, Devon and Cornwall. Grudgingly the State pays them dole but urges them to move, leaving their families and community, to go and live in strange and unwelcoming towns where they might find work. Those that refuse to move end up on the capitalists' scrap heap – poor, eventually unemployable, a burden to the State etc. etc. Not only are people expected to be geographically mobile, they are also expected to be 'socially mobile'. That is, through hard

233

work, extended education and a willingness to move frequently, people can hope to rise out of their class and enjoy the dubious trappings of more money and status. But to do it they must break links with their background, reject their families and class in order to identify with the class they are aspiring to. Just as the State requires people to uproot themselves in its service, so industrial organisations require their high status employees to go where the organisation dictates. Many professions too require a permanent readiness to move. The career teacher, doctor or scientist will find promotion blocked if she or he has an aged parent to care for, who doesn't want to move. Until the peak of consultant, professor or headmistress is reached, at least five yearly changes of job are essential.

As long as the worker is willing to sacrifice such considerations and as long as his first loyalty is to improving his own lifestyle, his mobility is guaranteed. If his first loyalty is to his community and not his pocket, then he is capitalism's lost cause.

That the extended family is now nothing more than a quaint anachronism, surviving in a few 'backward' pockets of industrial society, is an indication of how effective capitalism is when it invades what we regard as the personal domain. But while the mobility of the worker is fairly easily assured, his docility is not. The most a worker can travel with, without becoming a burden on the State, is that which will keep him happy, fed, clothed, rewarded for his labours, work fixated, satisfied and perpetuated, i.e. wife and children. Too many single men who can afford easily to go on strike, who are without the stabilising influence of home and small dependent family, whose mobility, instead of being useful to the system becomes a threat, would not be sufficiently docile, or malleable. (e.g. Irish building

234

workers who fiddle the system by moving on before tax authorities can catch up with them, barrow boys, market tradespeople and so on). There is a place in the industrial economy for temporary low paid work, with little loyalty demanded of its workers, who may be laid off whenever market forces require that they should be and who can easily be replaced – workers whose first identification is not with work but with their families – the actual reverse of everything I have so far said, and that place is filled by *women*.

For the purposes of capitalist economy then, the very best arrangement a man can make, regardless of his class or education is to:

1. take a wife who will care for him and see to all his needs and bear and rear his children
2. live with them in a small isolated group and preferably away from his first family with whom his links must be only nominal (aged parents are a liability!)
3. be intent on improving his standard of living, thereby committing himself to overtime or professional ladder climbing, both of which require long hours away from home and a patient uncomplaining wife
4. be prepared to move house and town from time to time but not to strike
5. support a wife and growing family.

For the purposes of capitalism, the best arrangements a woman can make go parallel to the man's. Her goals must mirror her husband's. She must be prepared to work long unpaid hours in the home while he improves his lifestyle. But as well as applying herself wholeheartedly to her husband's and children's needs

235

she must also be prepared to work outside the home for 'pin' money (i.e. low pay), but not to identify with her work role. She must only see her job as significant insofar as it adds to the family spending power and gives her something to do when the kids grow up. Her work must never give her independence, because his mobility depends on her dependence on him. Where he goes, so must she. So that if she is laid off at work or is subjected to bad working conditions and pay, it will not matter too much. Thus, two basic needs of capitalism are met. A motivated, mobile work force and a secondary, casual work force.

The small nuclear family, based on these fundamental premises, is tailor made to suit the needs of a capitalist economy. Though it doesn't always work satisfactorily (notably in containing the militancy of the workforce), no other kind of social grouping would come anywhere near satisfying the demands of our society. And so it is that (capitalist) industrialisation cannot co-exist with traditional family patterns and wherever capitalism thrives, so also does the small nuclear family.

Earlier I suggested some of the conflicts inherent in the marriage structure, conflicts which originate in an obvious paradox – that marriage is interpreted as serving the needs of individuals, whereas it is so institutionalised as to serve the needs of society. The same is true of the family itself, many of whose apparently intimate functions are, in fact, performed directly on behalf of society.

In many ways, any scrutiny of those functions focuses on the duties of the woman within the family. Her role hinges on twin ideals, neither of which are performed directly on her own behalf, but on behalf of her husband and through him, society as a whole. First, as we have seen, as a provider of her husband's (i.e.

236

worker's) physical, sexual, emotional and psychological well being, and second, as a bearer and rearer of children; bridging those two ideals is the casual worker – a role which serves both the family (by increasing its spending power) and the State, by providing a reserve of cheap, unorganised labour.

There is an elliptical line we can draw from the family through society and back through the woman, for it is she who underpins the most important functions of the family and it is she who is the victim of its inequities. It is she who, pinioned at the base of each family, experiences the contradictions. Over and over again, we will see that the functions the family performs for society are diametrically opposed to the needs of the individuals within the family. Sadly, because families and the women in them are divided from each other, these oppositions are understood as personal problems, inadequacies or, worst of all, an inability to cope. For instance, if we look closer at the family as a refuge for the (male) worker, we can see how, what is regarded as the usefulness of the family is, in fact, the usefulness of *women*.

Many investigators have noted, apparently without irony, that the average worker in the West does not get satisfaction from his work. So he needs somewhere to work out his frustrations, somewhere where he can relax in order again to be revived to go back to work, someone who will counter with love and deference the powerlessness, dog-eat-dog climate and alienation he experiences at work. Somewhere, in short, where he can 'be himself'. And so a wife, home and family are coldly referred to as the container for the worker's dehumanisation, an outlet for the brutalising effects of work which might otherwise be directed back into it. (A worker can punch his wife but not his boss!) A wife and home siphon off the discontents which, if left untreated, would endanger his continued exploitation at work and threaten the very foundations of the production process. We ought not to be surprised that this knowledge has proved useful for planners, industrialists and some of the sociologists in their pay. For instance, it is now common practice to vet the wives of white collar employees, to make sure that they do not have careers or personal interests which might get in the way of their vital role as a safety net for their husbands. Ideally, nothing should interfere with her ability or her willingness to be constantly at her husband's disposal so that she can accommodate his every need. It has been recognised as so important that the wife of a candidate for a job merits almost as much interest as the man and there are now independent agencies whose sole task it is to make discreet enquiries of neighbours and friends as to the suitability of the wife for her husband's job. Just how long it will be before the manual labourer's wife is also investigated before her husband is given a job is a matter for speculation, but the practice is already filtering down from the high powered, managerial level to the junior executive and senior clerk levels.

This is how Wm. Goode refers, in passing, to the usefulness of the family (i.e. woman) in containing the 'problem':

❛The conjugal emphasis on emotionality within the family also serves somewhat the needs of industrialism. At lower job levels the worker experiences little intrinsic job satisfaction; at higher levels he obtains more job satisfaction but is also subject to rather greater demands. At any level, the enterprise has no responsibility for the emotional input–output balance of the individual; this is solely the responsibility of the family, in the sense that there is nowhere else for it to go. The small family, then, deals with a problem which the industrial system cannot handle. **❯**

Thus the family is held to be the 'emotional input-output balance' for *men*. What Goode and every other sociologist of the family overlook is that women are also workers, that the lack of job satisfaction experienced by women is at least as bad and often far worse than the man's. Not only is she burdened with the alienation of her outside work but the home, instead of being a place where she can relax and work it all out, is a psychological treadmill in which she must put aside her own needs in order to smooth away her husband's discontents.

Much of the resistance to women's going out to work and equal pay and opportunities, stems from this fundamental function they perform; for nothing must detract from the prime task of seeing to the male worker's needs. Come rain, shine or disaster, she must be there when he comes in from work, he must have his meal ready when he wants it, his clothes washed, aired and ironed, his housework done, his children cared for and most important, a willing ear for all his troubles. In this sense, the family is only understood as beneficial to men; if women work outside the home (and most do), their wifely duties must always take precedence. That there is nowhere and no-one to siphon off the woman's work alienation does not find its way into literature on the family.

Neither, unfortunately, does it find its way into the forefront of women's consciousness. Day in and day out millions of women enact the same drama, never really knowing why they and they alone should pour their energies into damming up the harbour walls, while gradually and imperceptibly getting swallowed up by the waves which they are so desperately trying to fend off. Because it is an acquired 'second nature' for women to be torn two ways at once, the conflicts mostly go unrecognised, only emerging, in times of impossible stress, as 'neuroticism' in the doctor's surgery. (Increasingly though, through the impact of the Women's Liberation Movement, women can recognise that what they have always regarded as a private family problem, unique to themselves and their husbands, is in fact a social problem, directly attributable to the conflicting roles which women are constrained to play within society.)

How does the woman feel, being the vehicle for the "emotional input-output balance of the individual" (read "male worker" for "individual"). She may have been on the go since seven in the morning without a break, having got up, dressed and fed two children and husband, rushed the children off to school, then dashed to shop, factory or office job, shopped in her dinner hour, rushed back to collect the children from school, given them tea, sent them off to play while she prepared an evening meal in time for her husband's return from work, ready for anything he has in mind. (And that may be called a 'part-time job'.) She watches him eat, notes the furrowed brow, asks him if anything is troubling him, listens while he recounts the latest infamy of the boss/foreman/head, sympathises while he chews on, barely notes that he takes no interest in her work day, keeps a firm and repressed grip on her constant tiredness, asks him if he enjoyed his meal, then later thanks him for helping her to wash up. When he suggests putting his feet up, she says 'Yes, go ahead dear – I'll be with you in a minute' and while he settles down to the newspaper or the television, she gets the children off to bed and then slips down to the launderette. Like a puppet at the bidding of her 'second nature', she believes that rest and relaxation are essential for him but a luxury for her. She knows, too, that the strength of the family is her responsibility and that any complaint or serious demand for change would weaken it. So she simply doesn't 'bother' her husband with her own difficulties, her tiredness and her domestic work load because 'he's got enough on his plate already'. And it isn't 'right' for a man who's worked hard all day to support them, to come home to a complaining wife. So, with most of her choices already structured by her husband's breadwinning role and her own subservience to it, she tries as best she can to fulfil society's requirements of her and if she gets lost in the process, that's too bad. There are ways of living with that loss.

I have not, as some readers might suspect, exaggerated the picture in the least. My own inquiry into the lives of housewives (and my own experience), whether they were employed outside the home or not, revealed substantially the same picture as that revealed by two highly detailed studies. In the book 'Managers and their Wives', J. M. & R. E. Pahl document the relationship of men to their work and to their homes. Though the women are not the subject of the study, the pattern of their daily lives is just one long term of service and sacrifice to their husbands' work. One of their managerial respondents was asked how he saw his home and he replied:

‘A haven of peace to return to. Somewhere where I can get a bit of sympathy when I need it. . . . I haven't gone far wrong with what I've got; she's always there when I come home and always willing to hear my moans. She makes me feel wanted. I get a pleasant sensation from her at times. She helps me to recharge after hectic days. Basically what I look for – home to

241

me is somewhere where I can do what I please rather than what someone else pleases and my wife tolerates it; where one gets mollycoddled to some extent. 〉

"Always there when I come home", "always willing to hear my moans" and "where I can do what I please". And what's it all for? She satisfied *him* so that he, in turn, with his batteries recharged, can better perform the functions required of him by society. It is significant that this man prides himself on giving his wife a "free-er hand money-wise than some of my colleagues do"; thus, as Gillespie notes, he joins the ranks of the many men who accept the doctrine of equality without having to live it. A very similar picture emerges from the long study 'Sex, Career & Family' and shows that, if anything, the picture I have painted above is conservative. There is nothing to suggest that the men and women in these surveys were in any way unrepresentative of their class, and thus of millions of other families like them. In many of the cases quoted in these two books, the women went to extraordinary lengths to protect their husbands, and keep them ignorant of domestic problems and crises, merely in order that their husbands could relax from the harsh realities of their work. Nothing should interfere with the male worker's claim for rest, his right to peace in his own home. It is important to note that, despite the authors' sympathy for the wives of these men, the sacrifices of the women are only glimpsed here and there, being reflections of the men under scrutiny.

And the picture is the same across all social classes. For the functions that the middle class woman performs for her worker/husband are precisely those of her working class counterpart. Here the tensions may be subsumed more directly under the 'natural order' although the woman's subjective experience of the situation may be much the same. She too, is doubled up under the weight of the harbour walls which she supports unaided. Only the overt details are different, as the following account of a mining family shows. When it comes to the demands they make on their wives, the previously quoted manager and the miner have much in common:

❛Restricted to the home as they are, [miners'] wives do not appear *actively* to resent it. When pressed they will acknowledge jealousy of their husband's freedom, but many of them say that they find satisfaction in the care of their children. The husband having fulfilled his obligations when he has paid over the wife's wage, it is part of the woman's side of the bargain that the home must be a comfortable place to come back to after work, with a meal prepared, a room tidy and warm, and a wife ready to wait upon him. There must be no cold meals, late meals, washing lying about, or ironing to do while he is at home. These duties should be performed while he is at work; when he is at home the wife should concentrate on his comfort. The wife agrees with these stipulations (has she a choice?); both acknowledge that a miner's work is hard and that it is a 'poor do' if the wife cannot fulfil her part of the contract as long as the husband fulfils his. The authors cite an instance where a wife had gone to the pictures after asking her sister to prepare a meal and serve it when the husband came home. The husband so confronted threw the dinner 'to t'back of t'fire'. It was his wife's duty to look after him. He would accept no substitute.❜[1] (my parenthesis).

Thus it is not, as the sociologists have said, the family which re-charges the workers' batteries and contains his discontents, but the *women*. And each woman, in the isolation of her locked consciousness, silently and uncomplainingly carries out the duties that society charges her with, convinced that it is an intimate part of her married life, when in fact it is a vital link in the family chain on which the industrial economy depends for its existence. Exploited labour exacts its price and it is women who pay it.

Before leaving the family as a refuge from work, "the haven of peace", it is worth looking briefly at a new (or at least newly noticed) aspect. The latest function of the family which sociologists have unearthed is one that has long been known and experienced by women – that is, that the family is the centre for leisure. An obvious point, perhaps, but one that has been overlooked for a long time because workers had so little of it. But (with ecology/pollution problems permitting) a future is now envisioned where increased automation, shorter working weeks, longer holidays and longevity will make leisure a headache instead of a luxury. The prospect of thousands of aimless and under-employed men, crowding out the pubs and betting shops, wandering the streets is a 'problem' which is already occupying the attentions of government planners. As far as the State machine is concerned, it would prefer not to have to spend too much money improving social amenities and creating new ones, so the more the family fulfils this function, the better. I would submit, however, that it is not the family's function but the *woman's*. It is she, now, who is the sole guardian of the worker's well being and as free time is an important part of it, it is she who caters to it. It is not for her to poach on his territory and the best she can do is to care uncomplainingly for the house/children while he goes off and enjoys himself. (The 'football widow' is the modern equivalent of the colonial 'grass widow'). Again, what each woman regards as her private contribution to the well being of her husband is a common and essential feature of all families and is well documented by our planners.

The 'leisure function' is another example of the usefulness of the family for *men*. For there is no prospect of a shorter working week for women; no-one is concerned about automating housework or providing comprehensive day care facilities for children. The female worker, whether in her role as child rearer, husband supporter or factory worker – or more likely, all three – has no leisure needs which the family might satisfy. For there is no indication, either in people's minds or in the academic books, that the family is anything but a unit headed by a male worker with a few faceless appendages. The world of women in the family is hidden, ignored, abused and neglected – the forgotten underbelly of society, propping it up.

* * * * * * *

The Family is for Nurturance

THE one feature of the family which dominates all our thinking about it is its child rearing function. What other social unit could there be for bringing children into the world? So crucial is it to our thinking that, when pressed, we would say that child rearing is the very *purpose* of the family – the force which drives us to barricade ourselves in brick boxes, which restricts our sexual relations and which irrevocably seals the knot binding men and women together. So it comes as a surprise to learn that the driving force behind earlier family models was not solely its child rearing function, but food production, land acquisition, mutual support and defence. Rearing children was just a *part* of this process. These large households were concerned with mutual protection and survival, caring for the old, the young and the dispossessed equally. To single out the family's reproductive function, above all others, would be inaccurate and misleading.

P. G. Riviere, the anthropologist, contrasts our family model with others in the world and illuminates our single minded emphasis on the young:

‘It is claimed that because of the nature, particularly the slow maturation rate, of the human young, there is, in order to survive, the need of some stable relationship. Furthermore it is assumed that marriage is the only relationship which can provide this stability . . . it is not universally regarded as so among the peoples of the world. . . . It is an aspect of another very marked collective representation of Western culture which lays greater emphasis on the young rather than the old. Here marriage and its stability are defended on the grounds that it is important, even vital, for the young to grow up in a secure atmosphere. *That marriage is for the benefit of the young is by no means a universally accepted notion*; for example, the Trio Indians of Surinam regard marriage as bringing into existence a set of ordered rights and obligations which are mainly for the benefit of the *aged*.' (my emphasis).

As old people frequently remind us, we have no respect for them, we are not interested in their welfare and what, they say, is the point of working hard all your life if, as soon as you are too old to continue, people treat you as a burden? For the first and most devastating consequence of the small nuclear family is the screening out of the old. One hundred years ago, in an industrial town in the North of England, when traditional, extended family households were struggling to co-exist alongside the industrial revolution, it has been estimated that eighty per cent of old people were living with one or other of their children; now the figure is nearer ten per cent. Where once the family was a defensive unit, with the able bodied men, women and children working to support the dependent young, old and sick, it is now a unit which is wholly concerned with reproduction and consumption. The old are rejected because they cannot make productive (i.e. economic) contributions to society; the family has no place in it for those society cannot *use*. Children, though dependent, comprise the future labour force so effort, time and money spent on them is not 'wasted'.

We can see in all this that the claptrap spewed out by the media, women's magazines and so on, about the nurturant qualities of the modern family – the tiny enclave of love and caring in an aggressive materialist world – studiously omits to mention that the old, like children, also need loving care and attention. During

Christmas 1972 there was a whole spate of reports of old age pensioners who had died alone in their hovels, unnoticed and uncared for. (This, of course, goes on all the time, but such things make sensational newspaper fodder at Christmas time.) One women had choked to death trying to eat cardboard to stave off her hunger pains. The judge at the inquest indignantly remarked that such things shouldn't happen in a civilised society. His implication was that such things do happen in 'uncivilised' societies. The point should not have to be repeated but the fact is that such things *only* happen in societies which claim to be civilised, and only in societies where the small privatized family prevails over traditional communities.

I would submit then, that the corollary of the family's positive function in producing and rearing children is the cruelty and neglect of the old, thousands of whom are rotting away in State 'homes' or, grasping at dignity, alone in bed sitters. They are society's dispossessed and though their minds are strong and active, many thousands are condemned to live out their lives in mental institutions and the geriatric wards of dehumanised hospitals because 'there isn't anywhere else for them to go'. (It has been estimated that *three quarters* of the inpatients in mental institutions should not be there – their only crime is that they are old.) Though a great deal of time and energy is spent on assessing the deleterious effects of institution life on children, none to my knowledge has been spent on the old. The excuse always is that their lives are over. Perhaps we should ask them if their lives are over! What we do know is that their *usefulness* is over.

That many families do everything in their power to prevent their older members from being removed to the scrap heap is a testament to people's resilience in the

249

face of society's opposition. When that happens, it is not the family or the community which takes care of the old but, again, it is the *women* in the family. My neighbour, a middle aged woman with three grown up children, and herself one of three fairly well off brothers and sisters, gave up her job in order to care at home for her ageing mother. (She first had to take her out of the institution which the brother had placed her in.) Health visitors, doctors and friends and everyone else urged her to put her mother back into the 'home'. In anger she once said to me:

> ❝Honestly, they talk about my mother as though she were a dog that ought to be put down. I know she raves a bit and is a bit difficult at times, but for God's sake, she is a human being.❞

Do friends and neighbours go around advising mothers of burdensome children to put them in a home? (Of course, those children who will not lead useful, i.e. economically productive, lives – namely the retarded and severely handicapped – may, like their aged counterparts, be placed in institutions.) I know that under present conditions the care of the old and handicapped poses insurmountable problems and that many families do have to make an agonising choice between caring for them within the family or putting them in a home. But the choice is *imposed* on us. Housing, welfare services and incomes are so structured as to serve only those who will be useful to the capitalist economy – not those who present 'a burden'.

If we had more flexible arrangements for group, communal or community living, if houses were not built for the standard capitalist family, if society did not measure people's worth simply in terms of their earning and spending capacity, then the old, as *people*, would be indistinguishable from everyone else. No single woman would have to choose between a job or caring for an aged mother without assistance, because the aged, sick or well, would (like children) be a vital and integrated part of the community; responsibility for their welfare would be shared out amongst the able bodied in the community, just as it has always been in our history and how it continues to be in cultures where capitalism has not yet completely distorted humanitarian values. The more intensive the capitalist machine, the more people are graded according to their usefulness and the more intolerant we are of those whose usefulness is exhausted.

* * * * * * *

Producing the Labour Force

CHILDREN are not merely reared in the family, they are *processed*. They are stamped, labelled, educated and graded, first by reference to their genitals, then by reference to their class and then by reference to their 'intelligence'. To keep the industrial system going, and the profits flowing, we need politicians, businessmen, bankers, scientists, technologists and academics and, to keep them in business, we need an army of men to mine our coal, assemble our cars, build our roads, forge our steel and, to keep *them* going, we need an auxiliary army of women to work the service industries and to support the whole unwieldy edifice, we need those same women to care for the children, shop, cook, wash, sweep floors and warm beds. The family makes sure that the system gets the people it needs.

That girls are taught to model themselves on their mothers and sons on their fathers is a truism. It is the basis of most psychiatry and the foundation on which education builds. In this sense, the small family, unlike any other social grouping, is exactly suited to preparing the groundwork which schooling and social pressure reinforce and which the employing classes can then exploit.

Functioning people – that is, people whose personal needs and potential are sacrificed for the industrial system – are people who have internalised what Goode calls their 'role obligations'. The family has the first monopoly on teaching the young how to function:

❛Thus we are all under the constant supervision of our kin, who feel free to criticise, suggest, order, cajole, praise or threaten, so that we will carry out our role obligations. . . . Thus it is *through the family* that

the society is able to elicit from the *individual* his
necessary contribution. **,**

At every point in this process however, there are contradictions which each family tries to work through in its
own way. Our very first 'role obligation' is decided by
our sex and many parents find they have to balance the
needs and potential of their children with the demands of
society. And so, *acting on behalf of the capitalist system,* well
meaning parents discourage their daughters from enter-
taining fanciful ideas about being a doctor, vet or even
ballet dancer, not because they are intent on suppressing
their daughter's vitality, but in order to shield her from
future disappointment. Though they believe they are
acting only in the child's best interests, they are in fact
performing a duty which society has charged them with.
Society only needs a handful of ballet dancers and doctors
but it needs an awful lot of women whose life work is
caring for men and children, with only the odd stop gap
job in between.

The contradictions between society's demands and
people's needs become very evident in the growing
movement for 'free' schools. Here, teachers, parents and
children are rejecting the State system of education which
regiments children into those few who are destined for
'success', and the majority who are labelled 'failures' and
which instils values of authoritarianism, competition and
divisiveness in children. (I know a minority of schools
are making valiant attempts to resist these pressures.)
But experience in areas where 'free' schools are thriving
has shown that many parents are reluctant to allow their
children to attend free schools, where they learn according
to their inclination and without the imposition of
discipline and authority – not because the parents doubt
that their children would be happy there (indeed, much

happier than they are in the State system) but because the children will have to 'buckle down' sooner or later and the earlier they learn how to, the less of a shock it will be. At every point in the child rearing cycle, parents must abandon their beliefs about their children in order to prepare them for the realities of the society they will eventually have to function in.

The family unit, in fostering the age and sex roles required by the outside society, acts as a receiver and transmitter of the dominant cultural values. But, more importantly, the family is also the dumping ground for those values which the system cannot use for its own ends. While the family prizes generosity, concern for others, warmth and co-operativeness, the outside society does not. In practice, this means that brothers and sisters are encouraged to share and share alike and to be unselfish in their dealings with each other and their parents but because the family is a *privatized* unit, these qualities are only to be expressed within it. In its confrontation with other families, or with the alien world of work and school, then each individual is constrained to shelve his generosity so that he can put himself first. Building on this groundwork, the school ensures that each child will learn not geography, history or reading and writing, but obedience, competition and individualism.

Effectively then, the family produces 'functioning adults' – men and women who carry in their heads two entirely different and opposing sets of values. These values make an uneasy alliance and the only way they can be reconciled is by living a double life – surviving in the outside world and 'being' at home. This is a desperately inadequate solution to arrive at and it is men, more than women, who have to live it out. In the family-half of their double life, men are at pains (often unsuccessfully) to be themselves – that is to be loving, kind and generous, while in the work-half of their lives they are at pains (often unsuccessfully) to be self-seeking, competitive and exploitative. Many middle class men, judging from the previously quoted Pahl's book, 'Managers and their Wives', recognise these tensions only too clearly and are thoroughly disenchanted by the whole thing. Yet these are men who are thought to have made it, pillars of society and an example to everyone else. But, the authors point out:

> ‘They saw the difficulty of combining the ruthless and competitive values needed to further their careers and the gentler qualities associated with their 'real' selves.’

These men are deeply conscious of being rats in a rat race and human beings at home. The privileges of their middle class status – nice houses, cars and holidays – though a nice compensation, do not entirely fill the aching hole which such work creates. They would rather be whole men than half rat, half human. When asked about their aspirations for their children, so disillusioned were they with the trappings of their work and class, that many actively discouraged their children from following in their footsteps. The authors state:

> ‘Basically we consider that what we may be detecting is the beginning of a middle class reaction against competition.’

Though such signs are encouraging, we must remember that the more the family is strengthened as a refuge from competitive values, the more effectively are those values propped up. And increasingly, children are caught in this web of opposing forces. While parents pull

256

one way, investing a great deal in their children, depositing on them their frustrated ideals – the poor wanting to make their children rich, and the rich wanting to make their children happy – schooling and the work system pull in the opposite direction. However much potential for happiness and fulfilment parents see in their children, the educational system will grade them and line them up and send them off through whichever door the system deems appropriate. For the few, academic success and disillusion – for the many, alienating work, where any talk of 'human potential' is a bad joke.

Children are bought off by the family. Many parents make courageous attempts to balance these opposing forces, by buying their children's happiness. Recognising that their children are going to have to scratch, work and struggle for the whole of their adult lives, parents see childhood as sacrosanct – a time when the very last ounce of pleasure and freedom should be wrung out of their world. And whether it is in the form of expensive clothes, elaborate toys, or hefty pocket money, the prevailing notion across all the classes is that children ought never to be in want. The contradictions are not resolved, but the family does its best to equip children for the alien world they will enter.

Each family, acting as a transmitter, screens out those values and cultural expectations which are inappropriate. Because so much of the child's experience of the world is structured through his family and, more importantly, through the family's relationship to the outside world, the child learns its place. Thus, middle class values of personal development are largely unintelligible to children from working class families, whose energies must be wholly concerned with getting a living wage and escaping from the dehumanisation it causes.

257

And the middle class boy (not girl) learns to avoid physical labour unless it is in the cause of relaxation (gardening). It is because the family is such a tightly knit and inward looking unit that these values are mutually exclusive and that the divisions between the classes and the sexes go unchallenged. Until the doors of every family are opened, until the inner conflicts played out in each one are exposed for joint examination, the barriers between the sexes and the classes will not be torn down.

* * * * * * * *

The Family as a Consumer Repository

*"There is general agreement that the basic functions
reserved for the family are procreation, status placement,
biological and emotional maintenance and socialisation."*[1]

THE sociologists' 'objective' terminology hides a host
of meaning. We can translate their terms thus:

'procreation'	producing the next labour force.
'status placement'	learning and accepting your place, which is determined by your age, sex and class.
'biological and emotional maintenance'	servicing worker's physical needs and confining his tensions to the home where they won't interfere with the real world.
'socialisation'	knocking the best out of children so that they will adapt to the system and their 'role obligation'.

To this list we can add consumerism. Of all the demands
that capitalism makes on the family, this one has become,
in the last thirty years or so, the driving force behind
society and the family. It is the one function of the family
which investigators deliberately omit when they discuss
the family's 'basic functions', but the one which industrialists, planners, law makers, manufacturers, politicians
and advertisers treasure above all else. For capitalism
demands that each family barricade itself in a small house
or flat in order to fill it with largely superfluous and
quickly obsolescent goods, gadgets, furniture, appliances,
cars and assorted hardware.

Evelyn Sullerot noted that the consumer function
of the family hinges on the woman's role within it:

❛Far from being an earner through her production in the home, she has become a spender in her demand for costly domestic appliances. Instead of reducing the household budget by her activity, she now increases it.❜

And the commercial propaganda ensures that she will continue to increase it by exploiting the contradictions in her role – her insecurities and feelings of housewifely inferiority; and the media habit of constantly referring to 'the housewife' instead of the consumer (are women the *only* spenders?) guarantees her continued victimisation.

The small family is, at one and the same time, the dumping ground for surplus goods and the central pivot of the capitalist machine. Michelene Wandor wrote:

❛The family is a consumer repository; a high percentage of consumer goods is shovelled into the family; each family needs its own washing machine – not in order to reduce work and be more efficient, but in order to make more money for a few shrewd manipulators. . . . The treadmill of over-production, in order to make high profits for the few at the expense of the many, means that the backdrop to the projection of the Sunday supplement family dream is discontent. For consumer goods to keep moving desire must go hand in hand with discontent; discontent with your situation can be assuaged by the acquisition of this or that product, this or that relationship.❜[2]

And if the family is, as many women know it, a prison, then, says the dream, give it fitted carpets so that it will be easier to bear.

We live, we are told, in an era of highly sophisticated technology, yet our living arrangements are antediluvian. For the technology is not used for the benefit of the people but for speculators and 'shrewd manipulators' so that, instead of technology being harnessed to serve people's needs, it is manipulated in order to devise ever more ingenious techniques for building in obsolescence, massacring the environment and draining our only reserves of raw material in order to yield short term gain for the few. It ensures a steady flow of money from the family into the pockets of share-holders, stockbrokers and gross industrial monopolies.

We have only to look at a tower block of council flats with 80 homes, each one of which will have its washing machine, hoover, television, radio, iron, ironing board, private kitchen with assorted gadgets etc. Now we have the technology to collectivise and eradi-cate most of the menial tasks which each woman in each flat performs in isolation from every other. We have the technology for a shute in each flat which would carry everyone's dirty washing to a central automated area in the basement which would wash, dry, air and iron those clothes and return them. But the market for 80 washing machines, automatic dryers, irons and ironing boards is eliminated at one blow and so also is the alienated labour of the woman, standing mindlessly over the machine which 'eases' her labour. Or, if that sounds too horrifically 1984-ish, what about a single large utility room for each block of flats, containing maybe three or four large washing and drying machines. But our crazy system guarantees that 80 families will buy a washing machine in order for each one to stand idle 90% of its time. And, as often as not, the 'automatic' washing machine breaks down at the touch of a button so that the owner, having already shelled out £100 for the wonder of the age, finds herself paying another £5 for a new washer or

261

gasket. It's not technology we're all sold on. It's exploitation.

We also have the technology available for automated cleaning. Some far sighted (but naive) people in America devised a system whereby each home could be equipped with a suction device – not unlike air conditioning – which would suck out dust and dirt automatically, eliminating the need for hoovers, dusters, mops, polishers and the whole ridiculous array of highly priced, but dangerous and ineffective detergents. The suction device was cheap and very easily built into each home, and yet the plan never got off the drawing board, for there was too much pressure from existing manufacturers who had their own ideas about the 'wonders of technology'.

Of the many more examples I could cite, showing how vital the over-spending of the family is to the capitalists, I will pick out one which I believe to be very important. In 1970, a Yorkshire firm of builders discovered/invented a new building material which would revolutionise house construction. Not only was it very cheap, *halving* the cost of present house construction, but its insulation properties were eight times more effective than any known building material – "a conventional wall would have had to be $5\frac{1}{2}$ ft. thick to match the new method". It was discovered that "the insulation is so advanced that central heating is just not necessary".[3] When these builders announced their discovery to the trade, they suffered an onslaught of pressure from heating engineers, the coal board, building societies, central heating merchants and brick manufacturers – all of whom saw their profits wiped out – and their discovery was suppressed. The company was effectively bought off and now produces conventional kitchen and bathroom units.

The family then, acts as a multiplicity of isolated consumption units and provides capitalism with an inexhaustible market. Wasteful production, in the interests of the few, is assured by advertisers who, feeding off women's sense of inadequacy, urges them that yesterday's luxury is today's necessity. Obsolescence is similarly guaranteed by producing new and shoddier models each year, so that the family replaces last year's outdated model for this year's newer, better and far more expensive version.

* * * * * * *

The Family or the Community

IF every family opened its doors and shared its goods with neighbouring families – if the cars, lawn mowers, telephones, cookers and so on which lay idle most of the time – were shared amongst several families, the market for capitalist overproduction would crumble around its monstrous head. And the family, as a privatized and self-absorbed unit – spending frantically in competition with every other – would be transformed into something resembling a *community* with shared interests and common needs.

We would not see, as I do every evening when I look out of my kitchen window at the neat housing estate across the road, five separate women cooking five separate meals for their families, alone in their kitchens, or, on Monday morning, those same women, with sad, blank faces, hanging out their washing, divided from each other by the garage walls which the architects have 'thoughtfully' put up between the houses, so that these neighbours can never see each other. Are those walls there to ensure their privacy or to bolster the isolation of the family?

Communities cannot, in our present system, take the place of the small family. For even if we break down the psychological barriers which separate every family from every other, we still have the almost insurmountable physical barriers. In a word, housing.

‘. . . the front door isn't just a few planks of wood, designed to keep out the rain and the prying eyes of neighbours, but a symbol of the division between two worlds – the outside, public world and the inside private world.’[1]

❝Your home may be the thickness of a thin wall away from your neighbours but you have to go through two front doors and a state of mind to get to each other. . . . We live in the houses that are available. We adapt to their inflexibility. (When did you last remove a wall for a party or a meeting and put it back the next morning? It's possible. It's even cheap, but it's not allowed; the building trade blocks any new housing scheme that involves too few basic units.) These houses, rigid and barren in conception and design, condition the way we live and then condition us to believe that the way we live is the basically desirable norm.❞[2]

"Two front doors and a state of mind" – each propped up by the other. The few alternatives to this increasingly sterile existence are rapidly being eaten up by the machine. Large old houses are either being demolished or replaced by ribbon developments of the standard brick-boxed house, or are seized by greedy landlords and converted into dozens of bedsitters, which effectively divide people from each other while reaping vast financial gain. Working class streets, where some semblance of community life still survives, are being razed to the ground while the people are re-housed in distant and inhuman tower blocks. In the town where I live there is a group of people who live in just such a street, where they have a small but thriving community. Their houses are scheduled for demolition and the Council is obliged to rehouse them. They have asked to be rehoused together, preferably in any large old building (of which the Council has several) where they can be near each other and can continue to care for each other's children, share each other's workload and depend on each other for help and friendship. Needless to say, the

Council cannot entertain the idea. "What if everybody started asking things like that?" What indeed!

I am not suggesting that people should not be well housed with all the basic amenities, but I am suggesting that the price society expects us to pay for those amenities is too high and unnecessary. For instance, the same City Council has built, at enormous expense, a huge housing development containing over 1,000 flats. Each flat is modern, easy to clean, has underfloor central heating, waste disposal unit and so on, but despite a lack of decent housing in the City many of these flats remain empty. Why? Because it has been built on the most dismal outskirts of the town, because local amenities are non-existent, (one woman without a washing machine has to take a 20 min. bus ride to the nearest launderette), because it has no decent play space and is right next to a six lane motorway, and because the whole building aches in loneliness. Some of the more militant tenants formed themselves into an Association to demand improvement – a community flat, – a playgroup flat and a nursery for the many pre-school children who are literally stranded inside the flats with their mothers. The Council refused, saying that it could not afford to lose the rents, while the less militant tenants merely moved out, forsook their underfloor central heating for the back-to-back 'slum' where they were at least assured of friendly contact with their neighbours, and a sense of shared humanity.

We have the technology to build for the people and not for the system. We could have 'dream' houses but they would bear little resemblance to the boxed semi, sandwiched between a motorway and a wasteground. We could have community rooms, shared washing and utility rooms, play centres, workshops, moveable walls, community kitchens, restaurants, nurseries and gardens or anything else, but such living arrangements would be anathema to a society which depends, for its life's blood, on the small privatized nuclear family.

But what about my privacy? It's the cry which always goes up whenever there is talk of creating alternative living arrangements. But such living arrangements do not impose anything on us – they merely *remove* the impositions, impositions which we are conditioned to regard as privileges. We live with the myth that the privatized family guarantees individual privacy. It's not true. The average two child family, living in a four roomed house or flat, provides privacy for no-one. In order to get privacy (read solitude) people have to go *out* of the house. The only escape routes in it are bed, or, for the woman, the small kitchen where she peels potatoes and stares at the grease marks on the wall, her isolation made easier by thinking of it as privacy. Adolescents can go and sulkily escape to their bedrooms while their father hides behind the newspaper *willing* no one to talk to him. Privacy is located in the head and within the small family, no-one can ever belong to himself.

The reason why people find the idea of communal living arrangements distasteful is because they conjure up an image of people 'forever on top of one another' – as though one could live within the small family without constantly tripping over someone's rights, ideas, property, physical presence or dirty pants. The need for solitude or joint, shared privacy in the communes and shared households of which I have experience is never confused with the spurious privacy of the nuclear family. For a real community is a place where people have choices and alternatives, where communal activities happily coexist with private and inviolate areas.

268

Domestic arrangements, too, are made infinitely easier, simpler and *cheaper*. Shopping, cooking, cleaning, child care and so on are fairly divided between the men and women so that everyone has very much more free time than ever they had before. Only when people need to shop and cook just once in four or five days can we talk about privacy for there can be no privacy without *time*. Within the small family, any talk of privacy for the woman is a bad joke. Working for 90 hours a week is not privacy – it's hard, isolated labour.

But we don't have to live in communes to subvert the family ideology. I know of a group of people who, though they still live in separate houses, do divide up their domestic tasks amongst each other. For instance, shopping is cheaper because it is bought in bulk and each family cooks for the other four once every five days and what was once a group of polite, though distant neighbours is now a small community held together by friendship, mutual interest and concern. Instead of being tied to routine shopping, cooking, washing, child care, every day of their lives, these people have taken the first steps in community living.

It is only when those first steps are taken that we can begin, seriously, to talk about privacy. For the inviolate privacy of the individual is constantly threatened and eroded by the demands the family makes on the individual and the demands that society makes on the family. Capitalism needs to enforce a vice-like hold on the nuclear family. Without it, the system would simply grind to a halt. Only when people are free to live with each other out of choice instead of necessity, when architecture is designed for people and not for the system, when walls move at the touch of a button, when household tasks are collectivised, minimised and the drudgery automated, when children belong to the community instead of their parents, when the aged are brought out of their concentration camps, when exploited wage labour is replaced by workers' ownership for social need instead of profits, when media pressure which urges us to drown our isolation in material goods is abolished and when the dream of mummy, daddy, nice house and car and two bright children is replaced with the reality of *people*, will we be able to talk truthfully about privacy, who we are and what we want to be.

* * * * * * *

Better Halves or Whole People

THERE are no personal solutions. As long as the majority of women are underpaid and overworked merely because they are women, as long as beauty, motherhood and housewifery are presented as *all* women's destiny, no woman can proclaim herself liberated. The meritocratic self-made man who pulled himself out of his class by his bootstraps is an example not of individual liberty but of exploitation. Instead of acquiescing in his own exploitation, he lifts himself up so that he can exploit others. Liberation is not the freedom to exploit others but the freedom to live without exploitation.

Television, magazines and the newspapers have taken the movement for women's liberation to their hearts, at once trying to contain it and trivialise it. Reinforcing the two existing stereotypes of womanhood, they characterise as 'liberated women', first the career woman, who employs someone else to do her housework, and look after her children while she herself becomes 'one of the chaps' in a man's world, and second, the woman who turns sexual objectification to her own advantage. The sexually free woman, who refuses marriage and adopts a pseudo rakish male life-style, is now, fashionably, described as 'liberated'. She is nothing of the sort; indeed, she is merely the reverse side of the career woman coin. Both have placed their heads in the only two loopholes available to women in a male-dominated society and both have had their voices, claiming that they were different from the rest of their sex, strangulated into pathetic whispers by loopholes which turn out to be nooses. They have not liberated themselves, but merely been tamed.

The Women's Liberation Movement is not and never has been about the amelioration of the position of women *vis-a-vis* men in a capitalist society. The Movement is not about achieving equality with men nor is it about women digging roads, doing the night shift or working in the Stock Exchange. Because the Women's Movement analyses and questions the very fundamentals of human experience – the division of labour between the sexes, the tenets of 'masculinity' and 'femininity', the sexual objectification of women, the exclusion of women, children and old people from the 'real' world, the Protestant work ethic, the distribution of wealth, the separation of men from emotionality and women from rationality, the competitive and individualistic morality which divides people from each other while propping up a capitalist economy, and the oppressive nature of a society divided by class, sex and race – the Movement, unlike any before it, confronts both the minutiae and the totality of human experience. For there is not a single area of human experience which is hidden from women. The tentacles of every aspect of society reach out and encompass them. Women know what it is like to look after children and old people without help; to nurse the sick; to work in sweat shops; to be catcalled or whistled at in the street and sometimes fearful of sexual assault; to be told that they are good 'for women' but not as people; to be dismissed as ugly or merely 'pretty'; to be defeated and victimised because of their sex but still expected to work twice as hard as a man, at the workplace and at home, and yet take home half his pay; to fear unwanted pregnancies, to be refused abortions and safe, healthy contraceptives and to face compulsory motherhood; to mutilate their bodies with depilatories, tweezers, cosmetics and vaginal deodorants; to have their vaginas instead of their clitorises defined as the proper seat of their sexuality; to see the private, weak side of public men and know that much of men's powerful posturing is a sham; to have their halting attempts to articulate

274

their oppression dismissed and derided and, often, to have their sentences finished for them by their husbands. And so women bring the actuality of their experience, pinioned at the base of the family unit and in the lowest sector of the work force, into a *political* awareness of the totality of oppression.

Sheila Rowbotham wrote that "the liberation of women necessitates the liberation of all human beings", which means, among many other things, that women cannot free themselves while men are enslaved, first in their majority function as waged workers, selling their labour for the minority's profit instead of social need, and second in their psychological adherence to 'masculinity'. These twin aspects of the male role oppress women and until that role is re-defined in the light of women's experience (though many men stand uneasily in the standard masculine posture), neither women nor men will achieve anything but illusory liberation.

The existence of an autonomous Women's Movement may represent a thorn in the side of men and a bonanza for journalists, but by its grass roots nature (that is, a Movement which stems from experience and not from theory alone), its insights into every sphere of life, its call to everyone "to abandon a condition which requires illusions" and its urgent reminder to existing left wing groups and Trade Unions that the working class is not an all male preserve, the Movement has taken the first steps in understanding the mechanics of oppression, it has re-appraised existing critiques of capitalist society and exposed the ideology which such a society spawns.

It is not within the scope of this book to set out a programme for change or to mark the stages which the liberation of women will entail. But women's experience has pointed out certain pre-conditions for their liberation. The barriers between the sexes, as I hope I have shown in this book, are located as much in material conditions as they are in the head. And so a radical change in these material conditions must go hand in hand with a radical overhaul of the ideology and cultural stereotyping which now separates women from men and women from themselves.

Sheila Rowbotham noted:

‘Such a change immediately raises the need to transform the whole cultural conditioning of women and, hence of men, as well as the upbringing of children, the shape of the places we live in, the legal structure of our society, our sexuality and the very nature of work for the accumulation of private profit rather than for the benefit of human beings in general. This is an emerging idea and the means by which it will be realised and the shape which it will assume are still not worked out. But the crucial feature of this new feminism as an organizing idea is that these changes will not follow a socialist revolution automatically but will have to be made explicit in a distinct movement now, as a precondition of revolution, not as its aftermath.’

The Movement has no blueprint for the perfect society but there is a consensus on certain fundamental pre-requisites for the effective liberation of women; there is, also, agreement that though revolutions in Cuba, China and elsewhere have made tremendous achievements in removing the stigma of inferiority from women, no so-called socialist country has yet provided an example of what the effective liberation of women will mean to the people.

One of the first preconditions is that the privatized work now done by women within the family must be taken out of the home and collectivized. Among many other things, this would mean that men and women take equal and collective responsibility for the care of children, the sick and the old and that nurseries, play and health centres are controlled by the people who use them, by the community. And with community controlled shopping, laundering, cooking and eating facilities, the role of the isolated housewife, servicing her family, would become obsolete. But there must be no question that "women are moved from a home kitchen to a communal one",[1] for the key to the liberation of women is an end to the division of labour by sex and an end to the inferiorisation of the work women do. When work is organised for social need, then prestige cannot be granted to people working on a production line yet denied to people working in the nurseries and kitchens. Indeed, it does not seem too far fetched to envisage a society in which people are not defined by the work they do, as they are now. The breakdown of the division of labour by sex might hopefully give way to a dissolution of the separation in values between mental and manual work.

Another fundamental pre-requisite for the liberation of women (on which women in the Movement are in complete agreement) is the need for them to have absolute control over their own bodies, which means far safer and healthier forms of birth control than are now available, and that the choice whether or not to bear a child is left entirely with the woman herself. And so there must be no question of women genuflecting before the agents of morality (doctors, psychiatrists, social workers) to plead for an abortion.

A socialist society in which women are liberated

from their traditional double burden is neither Utopian nor unattainable. For besides the technology which has yet to be harnessed to serve people's needs, we have all the ingredients stored inside us (as was partially glimpsed by the civilian population during World War II), though they appear to be fragmented and often atomised by the conditions under which we live. To realise that those conditions divide us from each other and from ourselves, is to perceive the possibility of reassembling ourselves into whole people and the probability of building a society which is geared to our needs. That such a society is not on the horizon is an indication, not of the paucity of human potential, but of the power of ideology and the reality of economic relations.

For women the struggle is clear. The woman who walks bent over because she thinks she was made that way needs the Women's Liberation Movement and the continuing support, independence and sisterhood it will give to her in her struggle to discover herself. The woman who knows she could walk upright wants revolution.

* * * * * * *

Notes

The bibliography contains full details of the books and authors referred to in these chapter notes.

Self Fulfilling Prophecy

1. *Sunday Times*, June 18th 1972
2. Wm. Goode
3. *New Society*, October 10th 1970
4. Ann Oakley
5. Ann Oakley, *New Society*, March 11th 1971
6. Ann Oakley
7. Angela Hamblin, Ultimate Goals, *Women's Liberation Review*, No. 1
8. Wm. Goode

School

1. *Women's Report*, Vol. 1, No. 2
2. Newsome Report on Secondary Education, *Half Our Future*, H.M.S.O.

Toys, Books and Television

1. *Sunday Times*, January 30th 1972
2. *The Guardian*, February 1st 1973
3. Jackanory, BBC TV February 1st 1973
4. *Sandie*, December 1972
5. *Spare Rib*, November 1972
6. *Fabulous*, February 10th 1973

Alternatives

1. Rapoport
2. *The Guardian*, August 24th 1970
3. TV interview following the demonstration at the House of Commons by Women in Media and other women's organisations when Willie Hamilton's private member's bill to outlaw discrimination against women was talked out. February 2nd 1973
4. Leonora Lloyd
5. "Secret memos aim to stop equal pay for women", *Sunday Times*, February 4th 1973
6. ibid
7. ibid
8. ibid
9. "The 1971 Census revealed that 40% of women with dependent children went out to work (compared with 26% in 1961) and *one in five* women were the chief supporters of their children." *Women's Report*, Vol. 2, No. 1. 1973
10. *New Society*, October 1st 1970

Identity

1. 'A Woman's Place', film made by Lis Kustow
2. *Woman*, June 1971
3. ibid
4. ibid
5. This quotation and all the following, unless otherwise stated, are taken from twenty three tape-recorded talks with married women in and around Leeds in 1971 and 1972. All the women were, as the press likes to say, "ordinary housewives". I knew two of them personally and obtained the names and addresses of three from mutual friends. The rest of the names and addresses were given to me by a market researcher whose sample was selected at random from the electoral register and she merely passed on the names of all the housewives within that sample.

   I was myself a full time housewife with a small child at the time and I introduced myself by saying that I was writing an article (which was then my intention) about what the housewife's daily life was like. None of the women I approached refused to be interviewed. On the contrary, they were very eager to talk, once they had got over their astonishment that anyone could seriously be interested in the subject.

   I had initially prepared myself with a questionnaire but soon found it quite superfluous. I expected to hear complaints but I never dreamed for a moment that I would encounter so much sadness, bitterness and disillusion. Most moving of all was the repetition, in every tape, of the women's willingness to take personal blame for their dissatisfaction. "It's just something in me. I can't help it." "It's my own fault. There's no-one you can blame, is there? *Is* there?"

   It was the experience of listening to the accumulated tapes and writing down exactly what the women said which finally convinced me that I could not contain all that needed to be said in an article or a pamphlet.

Status

1. Woman's Role, *Sunday Times*, March 26th 1972
2. *Radio Times*, July 28th 1971
3. Ronald Fletcher
4. Margaret Puxon

Division of Labour

1. Pat Mainardi
2. Evelyn Reed
3. Evelyn Reed
4. Evelyne Sullerot

Housewife as a Worker
1. Suzanne Gail

Isolation
1. Suzanne Gail
2. Suzanne Gail
3. *Forum*, Vol. 5, No. 2

Time
1. *Women Now*, Nottingham Women's Paper
2. Suzanne Gail
3. Suzanne Gail
4. *Sunday Times* Colour Supplement, March 4th 1973
5. Jan Williams, Hazel Twort and Ann Bacchelli, *Women and the Family*, in *The Body Politic* (Wandor)
6. Michelene Wandor, *The Conditions of Illusion*, an unpublished paper
7. Williams, Twort and Bacchelli. op. cit.

Redundancy
1. Suzanne Gail

Economics
1. Benston
2. A point made by Suzanne Gail
3. *The Guardian*, September 9th 1972
4. P. Blake
5. There are 213,000 single mothers living in poverty on Supplementary Benefits. Of those who work, more than half earn less than £20.00 per week. *Women's Report*, Vol. 1, No. 3 March/April 1973

The Rise of Motherhood
1. Ellen Adams, The Family, *Shrew*, Vol. 3, No. 4, May 1971
2. *Times Educational Supplement*, January 14th 1972
3. *The Guardian*, October 11th 1972
4. *The Guardian*, October 11th 1972
5. *The Guardian*, June 15th 1971

Maternal Deprivation
1. *Sunday Times*, October 22nd 1972
2. *The Guardian*, September 7th 1972 and other newspapers
3. Grygier

Childbirth and the Mystique of Motherhood
1. *Mother Magazine*, April 1972
2. Margaret Mead
3. *Mother Magazine*

4. Dalla Costa
5. *The Guardian*, August 25th 1972
6. William Tucker, *New Society*, October 12th 1972
7. *Times Educational Supplement*, January 14th 1972

The New Mother
1. *The Guardian*, June 26th 1972
2. Death of a Marriage, *Forum*, Vol. 4, No. 11
3. ibid
4. "88,000 women a year are said to need treatment for post-natal depression. . . . Some specialists . . . believe the psychological after effects of stress at this time are comparable to that identified in soldiers returning from combat and prison camps. A Welsh survey has come up with the fact that 65% of mothers who have deliveries in hospital suffer from depression in some degree, as compared with 19% who are confined at home." *Women's Report*, Vol. 1, No. 3. March/April 1973

The Task of Child Rearing
1. Thea Thompson, The Lost World of Childhood, *New Society*, October 5th 1972

The Ideology of the Family
1. Margaret Wynn
2. ibid

Monogamy
1. Death of a Marriage, *Forum* Vol. 4, No. 11
2. Dreitzel
3. Gillespie

Economics of the Family
1. Anderson

The Family as a Consumer Repository
1. Anderson
2. Michelene Wandor, *The Conditions of Illusion*, unpublished paper
3. *The Other Paper*, January 30th 1970

The Family or the Community
1. Michelene Wandor, Family Everafter, *Spare Rib*, November 1972
2. Sue Crockford, Nan Fromer, *When is a House not a Home?* in The Body Politic (Wandor)

Better Halves or Whole People
1. Margaret Benston

Bibliography

Anderson, M. (ed.) *Sociology of the Family* Penguin 1971

Papers referred to are: Klein, J. *The Family in Traditional Working Class England;* Anderson, M. *Family, Household and Industrial Revolution* and Sussman, M. B. and Burginal, L. G. *The Kin Family Network in urban industrial America.*

Aries, P. *Centuries of Childhood* Penguin 1973

de Beauvoir, S. *The Second Sex* Jonathan Cape 1953 and Penguin

Benston, M. The Political Economy of Women's Liberation, *Monthly Review*, Sept. 1969, reprinted by New Hogtown Press, 1973

Blake, P. *The Plight of One Parent Families*, Council for Children's Welfare, 1972

Bowlby, J. *44 Juvenile Thieves*. Bailliere, Tindall and Cox, 1947

Bowlby, J. *Maternal Care and Mental Health* W.H.O. Monograph, Geneva. H.M.S.O. 1952

Broughton, M. Children with Mothers at Work *J. of Royal Inst. of Public Health and Hygiene* May/June 1962 Vol. XXV

Dalla Costa, M. and James, S. *The Power of Women and the Subversion of the Community* Falling Wall Press 1972

Dreitzel, H. P. (ed) *Family, Marriage and the Struggle of the Sexes*, Collier Macmillan 1972

Eekalaar, J. *Family Security and Family Breakdown* Penguin Law and Society 1971

Ferguson, T. and Cunnison, J. *The Young Wage Earner* O.U.P. 1951

Fletcher, R. *Family and Marriage in Britain* Penguin 1969

Fogarty, M. and Rapoport, R. *Sex, Career and Family* Allen & Unwin 1971

Friedan, B. *The Feminine Mystique* Gollancz 1963, Penguin 1971

Gail, S. *Housewife* in Fraser (ed.) *Work* Penguin in association with New Left Review, 1968

Gathorne Hardy, J. *The Rise and Fall of the British Nanny* Hodder & Stoughton 1972

Gavron, H. *The Captive Wife*, Routledge & Kegan Paul 1966, Penguin 1970

Gillespie, D. *Who has the Power? The Marital Struggle* in Dreitzel

Glass, N. Eating, sleeping and elimination habits in children attending day nurseries and children cared for at home by their mothers. *Amer. J. Orthopsychiatry*, October 1949, XIX

Glueck, S. and Glueck, E. Working Mothers and Delinquency. *Mental Hygiene* 1957 Vol. XLI

Goode, W. *The Family* Prentice Hall 1964

Gorer, G. *Sex and Marriage in England Today* Nelson 1971

Greer, G. *The Female Eunuch* McGibbon & Kee 1970 and Paladin 1971

Grygier, T. *et al.* Parental Deprivation: a study of delinquent children. *Brit. J. Criminology* 1969 Vol. IX, No. 3

Jacobsen and Rosenthal *Pygmalion in the Classroom* Holt, Rinehart & Winston 1968

Janeway, E. *Man's World, Woman's Place* Michael Joseph 1972

Lloyd, L. *Women Workers in Britain* Socialist Women Publications 1972

Mainardi, P. *The Politics of Housework* in Morgan, R. (ed.) *Sisterhood is Powerful* Vintage 1970, Wildwood House 1973

Mead, M. Some Theoretical Considerations on the Problem of Mother-Child Separation *Amer. J. Orthopsychiatry* July 1954, XXIV

Mead, M. Contributions to *Discussions on Child Development* Third Meeting of the W.H.O. Study Group on the Psycho-biological Development of the Child. (Editors: Tanner, J. M. and Inn-helder, B.) Tavistock 1955

Morgan, E. *The Descent of Woman* Souvenir Press 1972

Myrdal, A. and Klein, V. *Woman's Two Roles: Home and Work* Routledge & Kegan Paul 1956

Oakley, A. *Sex, Gender & Society* Maurice Temple Smith 1972

Pahl, J. M. and R. E. *Managers and Their Wives* Allen Lane 1971

Perry, J. B. Jnr. The Mother Substitute of Employed Mothers: An explorative inquiry *Marriage and Family Living* 1961 XXIII

Puxon, M. *Family Law* Penguin 1971

Rapoport, R. and R. *Dual Career Families* Pelican 1971 (Copyright P.E.P. 1971)

Reed, E. *Problems of Women's Liberation* Pathfinder Press 1970

Rhodes, P. *Woman: A Biological Study* Corgi 1969

Riviere, P. G. Rethinking Kinship and Marriage in Needham R. (ed.) *Rethinking Kinship and Marriage* A.S.A. Monograph Tavistock Publications 1971

Rowbotham, S. *Women, Resistance and Revolution* Allen Lane 1973

Rutter, M. *Maternal Deprivation Reassessed* Penguin 1972

Sheridan, M. *The Developmental Progress of Infants and Young Children* H.M.S.O. 1970

Stolz, L. Effects of Maternal Employment on Children: Evidence from Research *Child Development* 1960, XXXI

Sullerot, E. *Woman, Society and Change* Wiedenfeld and Nicolson 1971

Toynbee, P. *A Working Life* Hodder & Stoughton 1971

Wandor, M. (ed.) *The Body Politic* Stage One 1972

Wynn, M. *Family Policy* Michael Joseph 1970. Revised edition
    Pelican 1972

Yudkin, S. and Holme, A. *Working Mothers and their Children*. A
    Study for the Council for Children's Welfare, Michael Joseph
    1963

Getting Married Family Doctor Publication B.M.A. 1972

* * * * * * *

For information about the
Women's Liberation Movement,
literature lists, newsletters and
local group addresses, contact:

Women's Liberation Workshop
38 Earlham Street
London, W.C.2. Tel: 01-836 6081

| Tues.-Fri. | 10.30 a.m. - 8.00 p.m. |
| Sat. | 10.30 a.m. - 4.00 p.m. |

* * * * * * *